PETER AND ALEXIS

Borgo Press Dramas by FRANK J. MORLOCK

Chuzzlewit
Crime and Punishment
Falstaff (with William Shakespeare, John Dennis, and William Kendrick)
Fathers and Sons
Justine
Notes from the Underground
Oblomov
Outrageous Women: Lady Macbeth and Other French Plays (editor and translator)
Peter and Alexis
The Princess Casamassima
A Raw Youth
The Stendhal Hamlet Scenarios and Other Shakespearean Shorts from the French (editor and translator)

PETER AND ALEXIS

A PLAY IN FOUR ACTS

FRANK J. MORLOCK

Adapted from the Novel by Dmitry Merezhkovsky

THE BORGO PRESS
MMXII

PETER AND ALEXIS

Copyright © 1981, 2012 by Frank J. Morlock

FIRST BORGO PRESS EDITION

Published by Wildside Press LLC

www.wildsidebooks.com

DEDICATION

To the memory of my father,
Michael Morlock,
Who was no Peter

CONTENTS

CAST OF CHARACTERS 9
PROLOGUE 11
ACT I, Scene 1 13
ACT I, Scene 2 20
ACT I, Scene 3 30
ACT I, Scene 4 39
ACT I, Scene 5 42
ACT I, Scene 6 47
ACT I, Scene 7 53
ACT I, Scene 8 57
ACT II, Scene 9. 61
ACT II, Scene 10 74
ACT II, Scene 11 83
ACT III, Scene 12 90
ACT III, Scene 13 95
ACT III, Scene 14 100
ACT III, Scene 15 112

ACT IV, Scene 16. 121
ACT IV, Scene 17. 123
ACT IV, Scene 18. 129
ACT IV, Scene 19. 136
ACT IV, Scene 20 141
ACT IV, Scene 21. 151
ACT IV, Scene 22 154
ACT IV, Scene 23 158
ACT IV, Scene 24 160
ACT IV, Scene 25 166
ACT IV, Scene 26 169
ACT IV, Scene 27. 171
ABOUT THE AUTHOR 174

CAST OF CHARACTERS

Foreign Minister
Princess Charlotte
Larion Dokoukin
Alexis, Tsarevitch (Crown Prince) of Russia
Afanassief, his valet
Peter Tolstoi
Peter I the Great, Tsar (Emperor) of Russia
Catherine, the Tsaritsa
Theodosius, a prelate
Servant
Kniaz Pope
Kniaz Cardinals
Ivan
Cornelius
Several Old Believers
Princess Marya, Alexis' aunt
Princesss Eudoxia, Alexis' mother, Peter's divorced wife
Prince Alexis as a child
German Tutor
An orderly
Kikin

Prince Dolgoruki
Peter's Courier
Peter's Valet
Afrossinia, Alexis' common-law wife
Guards
Courtiers
A herald
Priests
Father Matthew
Executioner
Doctor

NOTE

This play is intended to be played with props but without conventional scenery. Characters, when not involved in the action, step back but remain visible to give a suggestion that what is happening involves all of them, constantly. Peter occasionally remains seated or appears on a dais. Pictures of Icons hang from the ceiling, but they do not suggest a conventional set. Occasionally the pictures change, sometimes, but not necessarily, to indicate a change of scenes; sometimes, within a scene, to indicate a change of mood.

PROLOGUE

The Foreign Minister is advising Princess Charlotte.

Foreign Minister

The Emperor understands your religious scruples, Princess Charlotte. You are a Lutheran and the Russian Crown Prince is an Orthodox. Yet, we believe Tsar Peter's conception of Orthodoxy takes the form of the Lutheran faith. The Tsar has abolished the Patriarchate and, following the example of the Protestant Princes, he has declared himself Chief Bishop. Now that the Russians are reasonably taught and educated in schools, all of the superstitious beliefs, must, of themselves, disappear. In these schools the teachings are quite Lutheran. The monasteries are reduced in number. Miracles and relics no longer command reverence. Thus you may be at ease.

(Princess Charlotte bows her head.)

As to conditions there, it is true they are primitive. The Muscovites do everything because they are compelled to. Russia is a country where everything is begun and nothing is finished. Should the Tsar die, farewell to all progress. The Tsarevitch, who is to be your husband, is not as complete a partisan of the old ways as he is reputed to be. He favors progress, but does not believe in beating it into the people by force as does his father.

(The Princess bows again.)

As to his dissipated ways, it is true, he is a man of not strong character. But he is stubborn beyond belief. Since his father will not let him have his own way and live his own life, he protests silently by drinking Vodka, thereby deliberately unfitting himself for the role his father tries to force on him. He also gains popularity in this way. Our ambassador believes that once the Tsarevitch attains the throne, he will reform himself and cease these deliberate dissipations.

(Smiling) The Emperor hopes that this report will satisfy your scruples and expects that you will marry the Tsarevitch, thus uniting the two greatest empires on the face of the earth.

(Princess Charlotte bows in acquiescence.)

(The Foreign Minister bows solemnly and withdraws.)

ACT I
SCENE 1

The apartment of the Tsarevitch.

It is small, furnished with icons and various decorations of a religious nature. Alexis is seated in an armchair. He has a hangover, and is still dressed in a dressing gown and slippers even though it is late in the day. Larion Dokoukin, an elderly man, shabbily dressed, is speaking. Alexis is about twenty-five; his keen intelligence is somewhat dulled by drink and sleep. He is thin, aesthetic, and somewhat weak-looking.

Dokoukin

Antichrist is coming. He, the last of the devils, is not yet come himself; but the world is teeming with his progeny. They twist everything to suit his plans. He will appear in his own due time, when all is prepared and smoothed. (fervently) He is already at the door. Soon he will enter.

Alexis (sharply)

And how do you know all this? Of that day it is written "Neither the son nor the angels know." How is it you know?

(Dokoukin remains silent.)

Alexis (yawning)

Are you a heretic or a Raskolnik?

Dokoukin

I am a clerk in the Arsenal. An informer reported me for taking bribes.

Alexis

Did you?

Dokoukin

I did. I was not compelled to, neither did I do it for the sake of extortion, but in all fairness and with a clean conscience, being satisfied with whatever was given me freely for the clerk work I did.

(Alexis laughs at his naiveté.)

Dokoukin

People had for years been wont to give me trifling sums—in all two hundred and fifteen rubles. I have nothing wherewith to repay the sum. I am poor, old, sad, wretched, disabled, and destitute. Merciful Highness—protect a defenseless old man. I beseech you, Tsarevitch Alexis Petrovitch.

Alexis (warily)

Are you sure you're not simply an impostor?

Dokoukin (simply)

No, Your Majesty. (hesitating) There was yet another reason for my coming.

Alexis (impatiently)

Well?

Dokoukin

Nowadays, we of the old religion are hunted from house to house; we are insulted and outraged. We have shaved our heads and our beards, we have been basely defiled. We have accepted strange Western ways. We have mingled with foreign heretics and schismatics. The heart is troubled. (passionately) It is dangerous to speak, but impossible to remain silent. O secret martyrs! fear not, rise valiantly and arm yourselves with the cross to repel the power of Antichrist.

Alexis (suspiciously)

What is your purpose in telling me all this?

Dokoukin

A little while ago, I dropped a letter like this in the Cathedral. (showing a letter and giving it to Alexis who reads it) But those who found it, simply burned it. Today, I shall nail a petition to the Cathedral door so that the Tsar himself will be informed. I write and speak so that the Tsar will come to himself again and amend his ways.

Alexis

Are you aware, old man, that it is my duty, as a citizen and as my father's son, to report this type of sedition?

Dokoukin

It is for you to decide, Tsarevitch.

Alexis

Are you aware that the penalty for sedition is death?

Dokoukin

For myself, I am willing to suffer for Christ's sake.

Alexis

Are you in your right senses? Think what you are about. Once in the torture chamber, you will be hanged by the ribs and roasted to death like Gregory of Talitsa who called my father Antichrist.

Dokoukin

We must all die once. Today. Tomorrow. What difference? With God's help I am prepared to give up my life.

Alexis (sizing him up)

Listen, old man, I will not report you. I see that you are honest; I trust you. (pause) Tell me, do you wish me well?

Dokoukin

With all my heart.

Alexis

If you do, then banish all this nonsense from your head. Never think of writing seditious petitions. This is not the time for them. If it were known I had seen you, I too should fare ill. My father spares no one. Go, God be with you! Don't come again. I'll put in a word for you. You shall be exonerated. Now, go—no, wait. Give me your handkerchief. (filling it with gold) Take this for your journey back to Moscow. On your return have a mass said for God's servant, Alexis. Only be careful you don't know who this Alexis is.

(Dokoukin stands with bowed head, in deep respect, before Alexis.)

Dokoukin

What else can one do but obey you? Who but you can aid us against your terrible father? Fair child of the Church...Russia's hope.

Alexis

Enough, enough, old man. Am I blind and deaf? Does not my heart ache for you? Should God grant me once to rule this country, I will do all I can to ease the people's lot. Nor will I forget you. Now, goodbye, Dokoukin. We shall meet someday, God willing.

(Dokoukin goes out with profound but clumsy reverence.)

(A slight pause and Afanassief, Alexis' aged valet, enters.)

Afanassief

It is time to be going. Would you like to get ready?

Alexis (musing)

I'm not going.

Afanassief

As you please. The order was for everyone to be present. Your father will be in a passion.

Alexis

All right, all right. But, bring me some liquor, my head is splitting from last nights drinking—

Afanassief (bowing)

Yes, Tsarevitch.

ACT I
SCENE 2

The Peterhof Gardens.

Beautiful classical gardens with mythological statues. Benches are set for a banquet. Alexis, Princess Charlotte, his wife, Peter, Count Peter Tolstoi, Catherine, the Tsaritsa, Courtiers and Servants stand before a draped statue.

Tolstoi

It was my great luck to purchase this masterpiece. The statue differs in no wise from the celebrated Florentine Venus and is in a better state of preservation. I had many adventures connected with obtaining this statue. (he opens his snuff box and takes snuff) In Naples, I was inamorata with a certain cittadina Francesca, celebrated for her beauty. (laughing) She cost me more than this masterpiece, and to this day, I do not grudge her a single florin.

(Peter pulls the cord; the drapes part, revealing a well preserved classical Venus. Peter holds the statue in his arms like a doll.)

Tolstoi

Behold Venus in the embrace of Mars.

Princess Charlotte

Were I the Tsaritsa, I would be jealous!

Tolstoi (reciting)

Cupid once upon a bed
Of roses laid his weary head
Luckless archer not to see
Within the leaves a slumbering bee!
The bee awakened with anger wild.
The bee awaked and stung the child.
Loud and piteous are his cries;
To Venus quick, he runs, he flies!
Oh, mother! I am wounded through;
I die with pain, in sooth I die.
Stung by some angry little thing,
Some serpent on a tiny wing.
Thus he spoke, and she the while,
Heard him with a soothing smile;
Then said, my little infant if so much
Thou feel the little wild bee's touch
How must the heart, ah Cupid be,
The helpless heart that's stung by thee!

(All present applaud Tolstoi who executes a faultless bow.)

Theodosius

This will not be a flattering oration, but I speak the truth from my heart: by Your Majesty's actions Russia has been led from ignorance to light and joined the throng of civilized nations. What was Russia in your father's day? What is she today? And thou, city of Peter, young in thy supremacy! How great is the renown of thy founder. On a cheerful site thou art erected. Verily, a metamorphosis hast thou accomplished.

(Courtiers applaud.)

Alexis

What a hypocrite! I heard him call this city a devil's bog not more than a week ago.

Peter

I am eager that the people should know how the Lord has helped us hitherto. Yet we must not slacken. We must bear any burden and work for the advantage of Russia.

(Applause from the Courtiers.)

Peter

The philosopher Leibnitz told me that science had traveled from the Orient to Greece, thence to Italy, France, and Germany and now is turning eastward to Russia. Now, it is our turn. The circle is complete.

(Applause.)

Theodosius

The Hellenes are not to be wondered at for bowing to heathen idols, but rather we Christians who bow to icons as idols.

Peter (as on cue)

There are many false wonders.

Theodosius

For example, the weeping Virgin of Petersburg.

Peter

Ah, I have it. (to a servant) Bring it here.

Alexis

This was well rehearsed.

(The servant produces an icon and gives it to Peter who

holds it up for everyone to see.)

Peter

Here you see Milady of the Sorrows. She weeps for our sins. See. Tears flow. But how? A miracle, perhaps? (pause) No. Two little cavities in the eyes and a small hole in the body large enough to contain a sponge. Presto, the tears flow. (he dismantles the icon expertly)

(Alexis has winced during this whole proceeding. Peter discards the icon with a flourish, all present, except Alexis, applaud.)

Peter

This is the source of the miraculous tears.

Tolstoi

I confess it troubles my conscience, in that being Christians, we worship idols.

Alexis

What idols?

Tolstoi

Why, this one—the Venus. They say there is no sin because these Gods never existed. But this is where folk fatally err. Because the ancient Gods do exist.

Peter

You believe in their existence?

Tolstoi

Most certainly. The Gods are evil spirits who, being cast out of their temples in the name of Christ, sought refuge in dark and desert places.

Peter

What the devil are you talking about? Excess of reading has muddled your brain.

Tolstoi

I have myself experienced the power of evil spirits. It was Satan himself who enticed me to translate Ovid and Machiavelli. Ever since, I have been an insatiable lecher and politician. And the Goddess, Venus, haunts my dreams.

(Everyone, including Peter, laughs.)

Peter

In what guise?

Tolstoi

In the guise of Akoulina, the dancing girl.

Alexis

No doubt it was she herself you slippery old lecher.

(More laughter and applause.)

Peter

Zoon! (Peter is using Dutch)

(Alexis comes forward and bows to his father.)

Alexis

Father.

Peter

Thank you, Aliosha. Thank you for the timber. It came in the nick of time. My own supply was lost in a storm, so, but for your thoughtfulness, our latest man of war would not have been finished.

Alexis (desperately ill at ease)

Always glad to be of help.

Peter (embracing him)

God be with you.

Alexis (abashed)

Thank you, Daddy.

Peter

You must stay for the conclave.

Alexis

Ah—

(A clown dressed as the Pope enters, surrounded by Cardinals.)

Kniaz Pope

Grace and peace be unto you, noble assembly. In the name of Bacchus, may the spirit of drunkenness be with you.

(All the guests bow to his holiness and kiss his ring or his slipper as suits them. The more solemn and outlandish a mockery, the more there is applause.)

Tolstoi

I propose a toast to the Tsar and Tsaritsa.

(All drink.)

(Catherine, Peter, and Alexis drink. A cannon is fired.

The Kniaz Pope anoints the guests from a brandy bottle.)

Kniaz Pope

May the drunkenness of Bacchus which passeth all understanding, in complete lack of steadiness and uprightness and sanity, be with you all the days of thy lives.

(Cannon fire.)

(The Tsaritsa, pulling up her skirt, begins to dance.)

Peter

Count Tolstoi, it has come to our attention that you have an unnatural aversion to oysters. Is it so?

Tolstoi (backing away)

I can't abide the filthy things.

Peter

Therefore, you must consume two buckets of them.

(Tolstoi bolts to escape but the Cardinals grab him and bring him back. A servant with two pails of oysters appears. Peter shucks one and dangles it before Tolstoi's face.)

Peter (laughing)

Open wide.

Tolstoi (through his teeth)

Never!

Peter

Will you refuse your Tsar?

Tolstoi

About this, yes!

Peter (grasping Tolstoi's jaw and prying it open by brute force)

For Tsar and Country, Count.

(More cannon fire. Alexis, who has been drinking, now slumps down in a stupor. Several persons are beginning to fight. Catherine whirls by in a wild dance. Peter forces the oyster down Tolstoi's throat.)

Peter (shucking another oyster)

One down. Only a hundred and forty-nine more.

(Tolstoi looks bilious and tries to vomit. More cannon fire.)

ACT I
SCENE 3

The other side of the Neva river, across from the Peterhof gardens, the same night.

A clearing with barges. Cannon fire and cheers can be heard from the other side of the river.

Ivan (singing)

A coffin of pinewood tree
Stands ready prepared for me.
Within its narrow wall,
I wait the trumpet call.

Cornelius (an old man)

Come to supper, Ivan.

(Larion Dokoukin enters.)

Dokoukin

May I join you, brothers?

Cornelius

If you come with God.

Dokoukin

I do.

Ivan

You are welcome.

Cornelius (suspiciously)

You come from Petersburg?

Dokoukin

From that cursed place.

Cornelius

The times are sad for fear that Antichrist is invading the world.

(Cannonading.)

Ivan

What hellish thing are they doing in the Palace?

Dokoukin

They have found a statue of a female devil and are worshipping it.

(They all cross themselves.)

All

Abominations!

Cornelius

The world's sands are running short.

Dokoukin

The Lord be merciful unto us.

All

Amen.

Ivan

I heard today, in the market, that there is no Tsar in Russia. This Peter publicly dances with foreign courtesans and drinks wine and spirits like a drunkard. He calls his drinking companions by holy names like Bishop and Cardinal to defile sacred names.

Dokoukin

It is true. I have seen it. And worse still, he defiles icons.

Cornelius

He keeps the true Tsaritsa, Eudoxia shut up in a nunnery.

Ivan

They say the present Tsaritsa, Catherine, had a lover. The Tsar beheaded him and makes the Tsaritsa keep the head in a bottle on her dressing table.

Dokoukin

He is trying his best to make the Tsarevitch imitate him, but cannot succeed. That is why Peter wants to rid himself of his son.

Cornelius

Lord. What trouble God has sent. Father against son—son against father.

Dokoukin

The Tsar loves foreigners; the Tsarevitch loves Russians.

Cornelius

Truly, The Tsarevitch dearly loves the ancient ways.

Dokoukin

Amen, amen. Since this Peter was sent to rule over us we have seen no happy days. How is it God tolerates so much cruelty to the godly?

Ivan

He is only a mock Tsar.

Cornelius

Three attempts have been made to kill the Tsar, but all have failed. Why? Because evil spirits attend and protect him.

Ivan (showing his hand)

See what the demon has done to me, brothers.

Cornelius

What is it?

Ivan

The Tsar decreed that recruits are to be marked by pricking a cross with a needle and rubbing gunpowder in it. It is the devil's mark. Try as I may to bless myself with this hand, I cannot.

Cornelius (excitedly)

That is it. The mark of Antichrist. It is written that he will mark them on the hand.

Ivan

Brothers, brothers, what have they done to me? They have spoilt a human body.

Dokoukin

He is the Antichrist. The beast feigns goodness that the people may worship him.

Cornelius

We must flee into the woods and the deserts.

(Sounds from the other side of the river. "Vivat, vivat, Peter the Great, Tsar of all the Russias." Cannon fire.)

Cornelius

That is the last of his signs. Antichrist will be glorified. Night will be changed into day and day into night. (pause) The only salvation is in death. Fiery death. We cannot escape the dragon. He has empoisoned the earth; everything is defiled. Everything accursed. We must burn, burn together to escape the poisoning.

Ivan

Let us each go his separate way to preach redemption through the Red Death.

Cornelius

Be it so.

All

Amen.

Cornelius

In the fire, purity will be revealed. We will be saved.

(More Cannonades. "Vivat, vivat, Peter the Great.")

(All cross themselves.)

Cornelius

Burn, rather than fall into the hands of Antichrist. One day, all Russia will burn with us. Women and children, too. All must burn to be saved.

Dokoukin

You are an old believer—A Raskolnik?

Cornelius

Yes. Already, I have preached the Red death for ten years. We have kindled many fires. Join us, God will bless our zeal and all Russia will blaze up.

Ivan

Then spake Christ, the Heavenly King. "Go tell my will to the faithful. Let them cast themselves into the fire for love of me."

Cornelius (fervently)

We shall burn like candles, a living sacrifice to God.

Ivan

Are you with us, brother?

Dokoukin

I am.

(More noise from across the river. "Vivat, vivat, Peter the Great.")

Ivan (low, keening)

A coffin of pinewood tree
Stands ready prepared for me

Within its narrow wall,
I wait the judgment call.

ACT I
SCENE 4

Princess Charlotte's apartment.

Charlotte is pregnant. Alexis is speaking to her.

Alexis

I have meant to ask you for a long time, Charlotte: do you believe in the divinity of Christ?

Charlotte

What do you mean? All Lutherans profess—

Alexis

I am not speaking in generalities. I once had a talk with the philosopher, Leibnitz; he shifted and shuffled, but avoided a direct answer. I saw at once he did not truly believe in Christ. Do you?

Charlotte

I think that Christ was the best and wisest of the sons

of men.

Alexis

And not God's son?

Charlotte

We are all children of God.

Alexis

And Christ is no different from the rest?

Charlotte

Why are you tormenting me? You know I'm pregnant and shouldn't be worried.

Alexis

Your people are wise, learned, strong, honorable, famous. You have everything, but you don't possess Christ. We Russians are poor, stupid, naked, drunk, repulsive—we are worse than barbarians, worse than beasts: But we have our Christ with us. He saves us because we cannot save ourselves.

Charlotte

You think you're better than all other Christians, don't you? You profess the law of love, but you practice cruelties not met with anywhere else in the world.

Alexis

To our shame, that is true.

Charlotte

For example, the Assembly last night was just like one would meet in Paris or London. Count Tolstoi spoke to me in French and Italian. All very elegant. Yet, from the windows, you could see the heads of the Old Believers on poles.

Alexis

What you say is true. But, one day Russia will unite Europe and Asia in a true Christian Faith. I, I will do it.

Charlotte

You! If you're so brave, why don't you persuade your father to take down those heads?

ACT I
SCENE 5

Aunt Marya's apartment.

Many icons and candles are present.

Alexis (enters)

Greetings, Aunt Marya.

Marya (a shriveled old woman in traditional garb)

It is good of you to come to me. Peter allows me few visitors.

Alexis (eagerly)

Have you a message from my mother?

Marya (giving him a letter)

As always, Tsarevitch.

(Eudoxia, dressed as a nun, but with a crown, appears on a dais, as Alexis tears open the letter.)

Eudoxia

God be with thee, my son. I am grieved to death that you have forsaken me and never deign to visit me. I wish I had never been born. Shut up as I am in a nunnery with only the Holy Virgin for company, while my husband in the eyes of God lives openly in adultery with a washerwoman and makes men bow to her as Tsaritsa. Why are you so idle my son? If I were a man and my mother shamed so publicly, I would know how to defend her.

(Alexis pauses in reading the letter which has visibly upset him and turns to his aunt.)

Marya

You have quite forgotten her. You never write to her.

Alexis

I dare not write.

Marya (sharply)

Why not? And even if it did mean a little suffering, what of it? She's your mother.

Alexis (rationalizing)

I wouldn't be the only one to suffer. Father would take it out on my mother as well.

Marya

I have had a dream. I am sure that God will deliver us. You will see. The Tsar will die. Petersburg will fall.

Alexis

Old wives' tales. There have been many such prophecies and they've all turned out to be rubbish.

Marya

Wait. Our time will come. The people love you and drink your health. You are Russia's hope. Be patient, Alexis. The Crown will not pass you by.

Alexis

Have I not borne it patiently for years? Will this torture ever end? My head is always on the edge of the block. Why? What have I done to him? Did I not try my very best to please him? When I was quite small, he used to drag me about on campaigns and I had to do sentry duty in the coldest weather and drink Vodka until my head swam. Is it any wonder I am a drunkard? And he is always angry and looks fierce as a beast. If you tear yourself in two, all he would say is why not in four? All right, all right, granted, I disappoint him. But I am not a fool and he knows it. I live according to my own lights, not his. He cares nothing for the people, I sympathize with them. That is why I am in disgrace.

—Do not do good, do as I will—that's his maxim.

Marya

Poor Alexis.

Alexis

And, it's getting worse. In the old days he used to beat me. But, do you know what he does now? He doesn't beat me or scold me—all he does is stare at me in silence. I talk to him and he just looks past me as if I don't exist. And this lasts for weeks, months. Is this fair? Better kill me. Lord, what is he trying to do to me? What?

Marya

Don't be fainthearted, Tsarevitch. Finish your mother's letter.

(Alexis reads, Eudoxia speaks.)

Eudoxia

Yesterday, I had a dream. I was lying in bed asleep. Suddenly, the door was thrown open and a tall, stout man came in with a foreign coat and pipe. He was clean shaven, but he had whiskers. Whiskers like a cat. I tried to cross myself, but I couldn't lift my hand. I tried to recite a prayer, but my tongue was dry and would not move. I glanced at the icon, but the image was no longer that of the blessed Virgin, but that of an unclean German harlot. "You are sorely ill, Eudoxia, would you like me to send for my doctor? Why are you staring at me, don't you recognize me?" I told the devil there was no mistaking who he was. Upon this, he grinned like an old tom cat. "You are quite mad, I am the divinely anointed Tsar of all the Russias, your former husband." I knew it was a dream, so I said, "If you are the Tsar, what is your name?" "Peter is my name," he answered. "Satan, get away from me," I cried. I cursed him. When the vision disappeared, I woke up. And I knew. I remembered the scripture: "There shall come a proud prince of this world under the name of Simon Peter, who shall be the Antichrist." Do you hear: his name is Peter. It is he, himself, no doubt! Peter, the Antichrist. God save us all!

(Alexis listens as if stunned.)

Alexis

I must not listen to this. I must burn this letter. Burn it.

(Alexis rushes to the fire and throws the letter in as if it burned him to hold it.)

ACT I
SCENE 6

Alexis lies on his bed, dreaming.

Peter appears on his dais with Alexis as a child, Aunt Marya, and the German Tutor.

Young Alexis

Daddy, you have a funny mustache.

(Peter bends and kisses the boy.)

Young Alexis

Daddy, why are your hands so hard?

Peter

I've been building ships beyond the seas. Wait until you grow up a bit. I'll take you with me. Would you like that?

Alexis

Yes, I want to be with Daddy always.

Peter

But Auntie will be all alone. Won't you be sorry for her?

Young Alexis

Yes. I'll be sorry for Auntie.

Peter

Who do you love more, Auntie or Daddy?

Alexis (shyly)

I love Daddy more than anyone.

(The German Tutor comes forward.)

Tutor

Method of instruction for the Tsarevitch. A syllabus to which he who shall be entrusted with the education of the Tsarevitch must conform. In his feelings and heart, at all times, implant and strengthen love for virtue, adequately represent the repulsiveness and consequences of sin. Use examples from history and scripture. Also instruct in the French language. Develop a good Russian style. Perfect him in general knowledge such as the use of compasses, science, and fortifications.

Children must above all greatly honor their father. When a son receives instruction from his father, he should always stand with his hat in his hand. When a son meets his father, he ought to stop at a distance of three paces.

Peter

Son, the reason I took you with me on this campaign was to show you that I shrink from neither toils nor dangers. Shun no toil for the common good. But, should you cast my advice to the wind, then will I deny you as my son, and beg God to punish you in this life and the next.

(Alexis, pacing up and down like a sentry, shivering, listens silently.)

Alexis

It's cold, cold. (crying, he continues to patrol his watch)

Peter

Son, we instruct you to depart for Dresden. During your sojourn to the city we command you to apply yourself particularly to the study of fortifications and languages. Inform us by letter when this knowledge has been successfully acquired.

(Alexis putters about rather aimlessly.)

Peter

Well, my son, I have reviewed your plans for fortifications. You have not applied yourself very well. In the future, you will study harder.

(Alexis begins to cry.)

Peter

If ever I said or did anything to hurt you, for God's sake, remember it no longer. Forgive me, Alexis. Petty annoyances are enough to arouse anger in me. My life is indeed hard.

Tutor

If persuasion and threats do not bring about attention to study, corporal punishment is fitting, even in a royal family. Use the whip, Your Highness.

Peter (angry)

My son, you have not applied yourself. I have beaten you many times, and all you do is feign illness. You are a malingerer. Beware, I'll cut you off like a gangrenous limb.

(Alexis tries not to weep, but brushes aside a tear.)

Alexis

I feel very sick, Dad.

Peter (ferocious)

Yesterday, you insulted Menshikov. I struck you then. Today, you shall stand before his rooms as a sentry for one week.

(Alexis paces up and down like a sentry.)

Peter

You raven, you starveling, how could I have fathered you? Your mother must have been an adulteress!

(Alexis jumps from his bed.)

Alexis

Curse him! Curse him, the monster, torturer, murderer.

Afanassief (entering)

What ails you, my Lord?

Alexis

Father. Father.

Afanassief

What can be done, my Lord? Submit yourself. It is written: "Honor thy father."

Alexis

Something else, too, is written. "Think not that I am come to send peace on earth; I come not to send peace, but a sword. For I am come to set man at variance with his father." Do you heed, old man? God it is, who turned me against my father! I have been sent from God as a sword, as an enemy, to pierce the heart of my father. I am his heaven-sent judgment. I stand up, not only for my sake, but for the sake of the Church and the people. No, I will not humble myself, nor submit, not even if it should mean my death. The world cannot hold us both. Either he or I!

(Afanassief crosses himself.)

ACT I
SCENE 7

Peter's workshop.

Peter is dressed in a leather apron and coarse homespun. He is forging iron. His hands and face are smeared with soot. The anvil trembles under his blows. An orderly stands nearby. Peter stops with evident satisfaction.

Peter

The bread will be long in baking. Before we can presume to teach others, we must learn ourselves. (wiping his brow) Bring my notebook. (the orderly presents the notebook) Make a note concerning the proper treatment of cannon balls. "To prevent rust, the barrels must be filled with fat. It must be ascertained with the help of a mirror whether the inside of the barrel is smooth, or whether the handles of the muzzles have flaws or bulge. If flaws do occur, their depth must be measured."

(Catherine enters.)

Catherine

I brought you some fresh fruit for lunch. Fresh strawberries.

Peter

Little mother, what would I do without you to care for me?

Catherine

Oh, you'd find another woman. You always do. Mary Hamilton for instance.

Peter

Oh, you've learned about that, have you? It was nothing.

Catherine (lightly)

I imagine it was. A little snip like that. But, take care I don't engage in "nothings" too.

(She goes out before he can respond. Peter laughs, eats fruit, and starts back to his smithy, but has another thought.)

Peter

Take a note. Since monsters or abortions are known to occur among human beings, animals and birds—and are in all countries collected as curiosities, a decree shall be issued to bring them to museums. Ignorant people try to conceal these curiosities, thinking such deformities are caused by the devil—which is an impossibility. Therefore, these deformities shall be preserved in spirits or plain brandy and securely bottled. A reward of up to ten rubles shall be paid for each prodigy. Can you work that up into a decree?

(The orderly nods.)

Peter

Good.

(Tolstoi enters.)

Tolstoi

Your Highness sent for me?

Peter

Ah, yes, Count. We desire your advice. As you know our son, Alexis, is a wastrel and I am getting old. I begin to believe I must disinherit him—yet I don't want to act without counsel.

Tolstoi

I believe your son is capable of reform.

Peter

Capable, yes. But how to get the son of a bitch to do it? I've tried beating him, threatening him—nothing works.

Tolstoi

Perhaps you must employ diplomacy.

Peter

Diplomacy?

Tolstoi

Confront him with no choice. Reform or disinheritance and a monastery.

Peter (musing)

Perhaps that might work. Explain your idea further.

ACT I
SCENE 8

Princess Charlotte's apartment.

Alexis is talking to Charlotte. She is very near her term.

Alexis

This is no business of mine. I do not trouble myself about your financial affairs. Especially after you complain to my father about me.

Charlotte (crying)

Are you not ashamed of yourself? Spare at least your own honor. In Germany, you wouldn't find a tailor who would allow himself to treat his wife like this.

Alexis

You are no longer in Germany, but in Russia.

Charlotte

I am only too well aware of this. Yet if only everything were carried out as promised.

Alexis

Who promised?

Charlotte

Did not you, as well as your father, sign the marriage contract?

Alexis

Hold your tongue! I promised you nothing. You know very well that you were forced on me!

Charlotte

I know you prefer that serf girl, Afrossinia. A woman you raped at knife point.

Alexis

Don't you mention her. I forbid you. (he jumps up in a rage, knocking over a chair)

Charlotte

A serf girl is the rival of a Princess of Wolfenbuttel—

the Emperor's sister-in-law. If only I weren't pregnant again I would leave this accursed country.

Alexis

Would that you would.

Charlotte

Go to her! Go to your servant girl! The father with the laundress, the son with a serf. Like father, like son!

Alexis (menacingly)

Don't ever say I'm like my father.

Charlotte (taunting)

Just like your father.

Alexis (lunging at her)

I'll kill you—I warn you.

Charlotte (darting around a chair)

You're killing me anyway.— You and your father. A devil and a devil's son.

(Alexis lunges again, but she eludes him.)

Charlotte

Only in Russia do they find two men like this. Like father, like son!

Alexis

I'll get you—you bitch. German bitch.

Charlotte

Go to your little serf Tsaritsa. Go tumble with her in the barnyard as your father does with Katrinka. Like little pigs.

Alexis

Damn you! (he rushes out)

Charlotte (drained)

I am doomed. This country is killing me. (she slumps down)

CURTAIN

ACT II
SCENE 9

Alexis' apartment.

Alexis and his friends are returning from the funeral of his wife. They remove their coats and hats.

Dolgoruki

Very sad about your wife.

Kikin

She was a kind lady. Especially for a German.

Alexis

She deserved a better husband.

Dolgoruki

I don't think your father should have insisted on being present at the autopsy.

Alexis

He would never miss an opportunity like that. Let us drink to her in paradise, but first, I need your advice. My father has sent me a letter demanding an immediate reply.

Dolgoruki

Let us see it.

Alexis (showing a letter)

I am at a loss what to do. Am I to become a beggar and hide myself among outcasts, or shall I flee Russia?

Kikin

Become a monk. A monk's hood is not nailed to your head; it will come off again. Meanwhile, you will have peace.

Dolgoruki

Be of good cheer. I have rescued you from your father's axe. There is really nothing to worry about. Write a thousand letters of resignation—renounce the Crown itself if necessary. Your decision is not irrevocable. Time is on our side.

Kikin

It is well you have not set your heart on the Crown. Gold is the source of many tears.

Alexis

Why won't he let me live in peace?

Dolgoruki

Does Peter let anyone live in peace? Is there a man in Russia who has not felt Peter's reign? And why should you, his son, expect better treatment?

Kikin

If it must be, go to the Emperor in Vienna. The Emperor has said he would receive you like a son. You are related through your wife. Or go to the Pope. He, too, can protect you.

Alexis

Perhaps, after all, that's best.

Kikin

Be not too hasty.

Dolgoruki

Your father is very sick.

Kikin

Did you notice that Menshikov saw fit to bow to you today?

Dolgoruki

The mice will bury the cat.

Alexis

He has the constitution of a horse.

Kikin

We had better go. We can be more use at the palace.

Dolgoruki

I agree. We'll postpone that drink till we have something to celebrate.

(They put on their coats and leave.)

Alexis

Afanassief.

Afanassief (entering)

Sir?

Alexis

Were you listening?

Afanassief

Of course.

Alexis

What do you think?

Afanassief

A bad business.

Alexis

If I flee, I will only be able to return after my father's death.

Afanassief

That's certain. But, how could you return, even then? The new heir with the Tsaritsa could prevent it.

Alexis

The ministers, the Senators, Tolstoi, Goslovkine,

Shaferoff, Dolgoruki, are all my friends. Baner in Poland. The Archimandrite Petchorski in the Ukraine—from the European frontier, all would belong to me.

Afanassief

And what about Menshikov?

Alexis

Menshikov will be impaled.

Afanassief (shaking his head)

Why talk so rashly, my Lord? What if someone should hear and report? Curse not the Tsar. Not even in thy thought.

Alexis

Oh, stop meandering.

Afanassief

I am not meandering. I am only speaking the truth. It is well not to praise the dream before it has proved true. You won't listen to humble folk. You heed only those who deceive you. Both Tolstoi, the Judas, and Kikin, the Atheist, both are traitors. Be on your guard, my Lord. You are not the first they have betrayed.

Alexis

I spit on them all if only the people stand by me! When the time comes and my father is dead, I will whisper to the prelates, to the priests, and the priests to their flocks, and they will make me Tsar whether I will or no.

(Afanassief remains silent, shaking his head.)

Alexis

Why don't you say something?

Afanassief

What should I say, Tsarevitch? It is for you do decide. But as for running away from your father, I do not advise it.

Alexis

And why not?

Afanassief

Suppose you fail? I shall have to bear the consequences. We are unimportant people, yet we, too, can feel.

Alexis

Be on your guard. Let no one know I told you. None

save you and Kikin, and Dolgoruki know of my plans. Even if you should report, you won't be believed; you will be tortured.

Afanassief

When you are Tsar, will you then also threaten your faithful servants with torture?

Alexis (ashamed)

Don't you know I'm teasing? I will do my best by you. But I will never be Tsar.

Afanassief

You will! You will! (Afanassief speaks with great conviction and fervor)

(Suddenly there is a knocking on the door. Alexis looks with apprehension to Afanassief.)

Alexis

What can that be? Can we have been betrayed?

Afanassief

Prepare yourself. (he goes to the door and admits the cloaked figure of the Archimandrite Theodosius)

Alexis

How is my father?

Theodosius

Very bad. So bad that we don't expect him to live.

Alexis (crossing himself)

God's will be done.

Theodosius (removing his cloak and handing it to Afanassief who exits with it)

Man is like a cedar of Lebanon. Yet he passes and no trace is left. His spirit will leave him. To earth he will return. God waits a long time, but when he visits, he is severe. The Tsar's illness has been brought about by his incessant drinking and voluptuousness. It is God's revenge for attacking the clergy, whom he wanted to exterminate. No good can come while the Church is overawed. Is this Christianity? Our Russia is doomed!

Alexis

You! You say this. You, who have been his collaborator? Where were you? Whose business is it but yours to stand up for the Church?

Theodosius

Ah, Tsarevitch, what power is left to us? We, who were once eagles, have become bats who flit in the night.

Alexis

It ill behooves you to talk, and me to listen. Who persuaded my father to defile the icons? Who gave him dispensation? (pause) Did he send you here?

Theodosius

Have no fear. I am not a spy. As for my actions, the worse, the better. Better Lutheranism than corrupt Orthodoxy. Let him convict himself. The cat will pay for all the tears it has caused the mice.

Alexis

Now this is adroit. You are sly, sir, sly as the devil himself.

Theodosius

Don't disdain devils. Satan serves God's ends even against his will.

Alexis

Does your holiness compare himself to Satan?

Theodosius

I am a diplomat. With wolves, I howl a bit. That's all.

Alexis

May I ask you, Holy Father, do you believe in God?

Theodosius

I prefer not to answer that question.

Alexis

Why?

Theodosius (smoothly)

It is hardly relevant. There is no God in Holy Church. So, why believe in him? But you, Alexis Petrovitch, are no fool. You are more intelligent than your father. The Tsar is clever, yes—but he doesn't know men. We often used to lead him by the nose. You will be a better judge of men. (Suddenly he stoops to kiss Alexis' hand. Alexis withdraws his hand as if touched by a snake.)

Alexis

Be careful, prelate! Don't overreach yourself. The pitcher goes to the well till it breaks.

Theodosius

It is bad enough as it is. I've always had a premonition that he will kill me. Always. He is called the Great! But, in what does his greatness reveal itself? He is a tyrant. He introduces civilization with an axe and knout. (sneeringly) He will force us to be free. He is ever in search of plots and rebellions—but does not realize that he is, himself, the source of all unrest. What multitudes have been executed to make us like Europeans. We are not Europeans. We are Russians. Blood is not water. It cries for vengeance. How many martyrs have fallen! Soon will God's wrath come down upon Russia. And only then will the Church rise—out of the blood of civil war.

Alexis

This is the end of your policies?

Theodosius

It seems that God will spare us. The Tsar is struck down. You are our salvation, you, most pious Alexis Petrovitch, Autocrat of all the Russias, Your Majesty. (he kneels)

Alexis (astounded)

Have you lost your mind?

Theodosius

Not at all! I wanted to become Patriarch. I renounce it. I want nothing. Everything belongs to you, Your Majesty. Restore the Church. Reign as Tsar and Patriarch. You shall be greater than any other Tsar before or after you. Restore the Church. You, the first, I, but a worm under your foot.

(Theodosius makes a profound obeisance and withdraws. Alexis is spellbound.)

Alexis (crossing himself)

Avaunt Satan!

Afanassief (returning)

Have a care, Tsarevitch. Your father is not so ill as he seems. He is only testing you—and others. You know the fable. The mice gathered together to bury the cat, when up leapt the cat.

Alexis

It's delirium.

ACT II
SCENE 10

Peter's office.

Alexis stands more or less at attention. Alexis is shivering; he is physically afraid of his father. Peter speaks at first somewhat mechanically, as if from a memorized speech. Peter is sitting in an armchair.

Peter

God is not responsible for your incapacity, since he neither deprived you of reason, nor robbed you of physical strength. Though you are not particularly strong, neither are you weak. Yet, you stubbornly refuse to interest yourself in military affairs or even administration. (shouting) Contempt for the defense of the nation will lead to general ruin, as many historical examples show. (lower) Perhaps, you imagine that generals can be got who will fight for you? Even so, they will look to you for an example. And if they see a shirker, (contemptuously) they, too, will shirk. Having no liking for military affairs, you studied nothing. (somewhat louder) Being ignorant, how can you command? How can you even reward the deserving and punish the indolent?

(Alexis twitches and squirms, but says nothing. He cannot speak up for himself before his father. This is part of the tragedy. His protests are silent, but no less eloquent for all that.)

Peter

You advance your weak health as an excuse! But it is no excuse. I do not demand superhuman efforts—only goodwill—and what do I find?

(Pause. Peter is beginning to have hard going. He would prefer his son to argue with him in a manly way. He is ready to refute all arguments, perhaps, even to listen—but there is no defense, no exchange of ideas—only a conflict of inexorable wills, one no less determined than the other.)

Peter (taking some water, waiting, hoping for a response, any response)

Having laid this before you, I will now return to your character—for I am only human and liable to die at any moment.

(Alexis starts slightly at these words and looks cautiously at his father.)

Peter

To whom shall I leave that, which with God's help, I have begun to plant? Shall it be to one who has buried the talent God gave him? I refer to your wicked and obstinate character. How many times have I remonstrated with you upon this? How many years is it since I gave up frequenting your company—but to no purpose? (Peter is now shouting at the top of his lungs)

(Alexis manages somehow to betray no emotion.)

Peter

You will do nothing. All you ask is to lead a life of indolence and self indulgence. (savagely) There is something in you that thwarts all my projects!

(Alexis still betrays no emotion. Perhaps, just perhaps, there is a gleam of triumph in his eye. Any other man, even Menshikov would have wilted under Peter's rage. Alexis seems to slowly stiffen throughout this speech. Alexis is no coward. As the test of wills proceeds, both his nerve and his will harden.)

Peter

You are surrounded by worthless people who can advance you in nothing except depravity. And what return do you make to your father for your birth? Do you help me in running this wretched, barbaric country? Ah, never! Never! But, what is worse, you actually hate my work, which I, not sparing my own life, have done for my people. Worse still, it is plain you will destroy everything after my death. Is it not so? (Peter breaks off in a fit of coughing)

Alexis (casually)

Can I get you some water?

(Peter, still coughing, indignantly signals a refusal.)

Peter

Seeing that I can in no way induce you to reform, I have resolved to declare unto you my last will and testament, and then to observe your actions. Therefore, let it be known unto you— (Peter breaks off into a severe fit of coughing. This time Alexis is agitated. He tries to help his father, raises his arms; Peter does not resist. The coughing subsides.) — Once more, I repeat, so that you may know—

Alexis (breaking in for the first time)

Father, God is my witness, that towards you I have been guilty of no vile action or design. I am unfit for the throne and fear to undertake responsibilities which— (his voice breaking) Oh, God—father—

Peter (moved, but trying to remain stern)

Drop this childishness! Prove your faith by deeds! I want no excuses. Words cannot be trusted. (beginning again after mastering his emotion) Idlers are not high in my favor! Russia needs workers. The Tsar must work the hardest of all. He who eats bread, but is unprofitable to his country, is like the worm who brings everything into decay. You have shown yourself to be an idler—

(Alexis winces. These last remarks have hurt him. He raises his hand in mute protest. But pain is succeeded by anger. He is ready with his retort.)

Alexis (icily)

Most gracious sovereign and father, what else can I say, but that should you, because of my unfitness, take from me the inheritance of the Russian Crown,—your will be done. Let it be so! (Peter is stunned) If I am incapable, find a stronger man than I. Thank God I have a brother. Therefore, in the sight of God, I renounce the Crown.

Peter (savagely)

Your brother is an infant! You don't mean it!

Alexis

I am prepared to confirm this statement in my own handwriting. I only ask you to protect my children.

(Peter is overwhelmed. This was not what he wanted. Alexis always has an infuriating way of holding his position. Unbending even while seeming to bend. Alexis refuses to be Tsar if he cannot be the Tsar he wants to be. He will not be the Tsar Peter wants him to be. He will be Alexis, not Peter.)

Peter

This is a trick.

Alexis

I cannot contend with you, father. I am sorry I have disappointed you. I ask only to be fed until I die.

Peter

Your resignation is only a means of gaining time. If today you neither fear nor respect your father's commands, how could you keep your word after his death? Your oath is of no value. King David truly said, "All men are liars." Even if you, yourself, desire to keep it, you could easily be influenced by the priests and monks who, because of their indolence and backwardness, are not, at present, highly favored. Yet, they are dear to you! Exceedingly dear to you! No—you shall not escape so easily. You must either prove yourself worthy of the throne or else become a monk!

(At this point, if the director feels appropriate, Peter

and Alexis place on masks. The masks may be removed or reassumed according to whether the two are acting honestly with each other or assuming a fixed attitude.)

Peter (savagely)

We cannot rest unless this choice is made, especially now that our health is giving way. Choose!

(Alexis remains silent.)

Alexis (aside)

Will he murder me? Does it matter?

Peter (screaming and pounding the table)

Why do you remain silent? (trembling) Take care, Alexis. You think I don't know you? But I do. I see through you, through and through. You have rebelled against your own blood, you brat! You long for your own father's death! Oh, you hypocrite! You cursed, sanctimonious humbug! You probably learnt such dissimulation from the priests!

Alexis (smiling maliciously)

Must I decide now?

Peter

This is the last warning! (evenly) Consider well. And

when you have decided, inform me. Should my finger become gangrenous, would I not be obliged to cut it off, though it be a part of my body? So will I cut you off. Do not think I speak merely to frighten you. Before God, I swear I will do as I say. I have not spared myself in serving my country, why should I spare you, you who are worthless? Better a good stranger than a worthless son— Either mend your ways, or become a monk.— Should you fail to make a choice, I will proceed to prosecute you as a malefactor.

Alexis (glibly)

I wish to become a monk, and pray for your gracious sanction.

Peter

Liar! Go away!

(Alexis meets his father's eyes. Peter suddenly drops his gaze, knowing his obstinate brat has managed to thwart him again. Peter groans like a wounded bull, then raises his mighty fist and hurls himself at his son. Before he can do so, The Tsaritsa, Catherine rushes in.)

Alexis

I will be a monk.

Catherine (coaxingly)

Peter, Peter, don't tire yourself. Don't excite yourself, my dear. (commandingly) You go, Tsarevitch. God be with you. You see the Tsar is unwell.

(Alexis relaxes his gaze and quietly exits, bowing respectfully. He has won a skirmish, but war has been declared.)

Catherine

Let me stroke your head. It always helps you when you are upset.

(Peter lies on the couch with his head on her lap. She strokes his head as the scene closes. One thing about Catherine, she has no ambitions. She is not intriguing against Alexis for herself or her son. She would help, if she could. She has no malice or jealousy.)

ACT II
SCENE 11

Alexis' apartment.

Peter appears on a dais at back with a courier.

Peter

My son— When I said goodbye to you last time, I told you to think over a certain matter. Think it well over, and tell me your decision. I have waited these seven months. Now you have had ample time for consideration. On receipt of this letter, decide at once. If you choose to be my heir, come to me at once. Should you prefer the other course, write me when and where so that my heart may be at rest. To this messenger, entrust the answer. Your choice, this time, must be final, for I perceive, that, as usual, you are spending your time to no purpose.

(The lights dim and Peter disappears.)

Alexis (to the courier)

Tell him I am coming at once. (the courier salutes and exits)

Afanassief

Are you going to your father?

Alexis

To him, or somewhere else.

Afanassief

Tsarevitch! How, somewhere else?

Alexis

I should like to see Venice. (hesitating) I only do this to save myself. Mind you, keep silence. No one else besides you knows anything about it.

Afanassief

I will keep your secret. Only we'll have a rough time of it after you've gone. Think what you are about.

Alexis

I did not expect any message from my father— But, now I see it is God who guides me.

Afanassief

Many in your station have sought refuge in flight. But it has never happened in Russia within the memory of man. (pause) What will you do with Afrossinia?

Alexis

I'll take her with me.

Afanassief (exiting)

Humph!

(Prince Dolgoruki enters.)

Dolgoruki

Are you going to your father?

Alexis

Where else, Prince?

Dolgoruki

Where else? Come, I'll tell you. Had I considered only the Tsar's temper, and had there been no Tsaritsa, I would have been the first to desert at Stettin myself. (the Prince presses Alexis' hand) Could I serve thee in any way, I would gladly lay down my life.

Alexis (fervently)

Don't forget me.

Dolgoruki

My cousin, Jacob Dolgoruki, sends word that a bad reception awaits you.

Alexis

I shall not forget this kindness.

(Dolgoruki bows and exits. A slight pause and Kikin enters.)

Alexis

Have you found me a refuge?

Kikin

I have. Go straight to the Emperor in Vienna. The Austrians will not betray you. The Austrian Emperor will receive you like a son.

Alexis

Should envoys from my father meet me at Danzig— what shall I do then?

Kikin

Escape at night. Never mind the luggage. If two envoys arrive, pretend to be sick. Send one back to Peter and flee from the other.

Alexis

Still—

Kikin

Remember, Tsarevitch, your father will not let you become a monk now, even if you should want to. Your friends, the Senators, have persuaded him to keep you always with him, hoping to kill you through exhaustion. Your father said it was well thought of. Further, Prince Menshikov argued you might live too long in the monastery. Knowing these plans, I am surprised they have not laid violent hands on you before now. They might, however, do this—get you aboard a man of war under pretext of instruction. The Captain of the ship will have orders to engage a Swedish vessel and thus get you killed. The rumor comes from Copenhagen, and explains why you are now wanted.

Alexis

It seems a little far fetched.

Kikin

To avoid the public disgrace of killing his mother, Nero built a ship specially constructed so that it would sink when a few miles from shore.— (urgently) Nothing but flight can save you. To willingly run your head into the noose that is prepared for you would be the height of idiocy.

Alexis (drowsily)

It's a big decision.

Kikin

What's the matter with you? Don't you feel well?

Alexis

I am very tired.

Kikin

One more thing. Should your father send some one to try to persuade you to return—do not, on any account, listen to him. Not even if he promises you a complete pardon on the most sacred oath. He will publicly behead you.

Alexis

I believe it.

Kikin

I must go.

Alexis

Go with God!

(Alexis pauses, looks about with hesitation, then, exultantly.)

Alexis

Freedom! Freedom!

CURTAIN

ACT III
SCENE 12

The Audience Hall of the Holy Roman Emperor in Vienna.

The Emperor sits on a throne flanked by his Foreign Minister. Peter appears on the dais with a courier. The courier delivers the message to the Foreign Minister as Peter speaks.

Peter

Most serene and mighty Emperor. I am compelled to announce to your Imperial Majesty, in fraternal confidence, with heartfelt sorrow, a calamity which has unexpectedly befallen us. It concerns our son .Alexis. We have grounds for believing that Your Majesty is not unaware that his past behavior was always in opposition to our fatherly will. Some time ago, we ordered him to join us on campaign, hoping by this means, to sever him from his worthless companions. Instead of joining us, he disappeared: no one knows where. Yet we have fatherly compassion for him. We fear lest his evil advisors bring him to destruction. Therefore, we pray, your Imperial Majesty, should he be in hiding in your dominions, to give orders that he be sent to us under safe convoy of several officers, in order that we may fatherly chide him for his well being. (fiercely) If you refuse to deliver him up of your own good will, we will seek him out by force of arms.

(The Emperor remains imperturbably silent. The Foreign Minister comes forward.)

Foreign Minister

The Emperor, prompted by ties of relationship, as well as compassion for the sufferings of the Tsarevitch, and by the traditional generosity of the imperial house towards all innocently persecuted persons, has granted shelter and protection to the Tsar's son. The Emperor asks His Majesty, The King of England, whether he, too, as an Elector and relative of the house of Braunschweigen, if he is also disposed to extend protection to the persecuted youth. His miserable condition and the evident and continuing tyranny of his father— including the justifiable fear of prisoners, should be sufficient to melt the sternest heart.

Peter (raging)

Is he my accuser? Is he to be a weapon in the hands of my enemies? Must I fear my own son? (pause) To kill him were too little.

Foreign Minister

It is reported that soon after the birth of the Tsarevitch, his father attempted to force his abdication. Several attempts have been made to force him to a hermitage. Then, a new plan was devised. He was to be lured to Holland under the pretext of instruction, placed on a Russian vessel, the Captain thereof, given orders to engage a Swedish vessel. During the engagement, the Tsarevitch would be killed—supposedly by action of the Swedish vessel. That was the reason for his flight. All Europe stands in horror of this barbarism.

Peter (clenching his fist)

All our agents shall seek him, and find him—no matter where. Spare no expense.

Alexis (stepping forward)

The Emperor must save me. I am innocent before my father. I have always loved, honored, and obeyed him. I know that compared to him, I am only a weakling. My tutors did their best to make a drunkard of me. My father used to be kind to me. But ever since my late wife began bearing children—the new Tsaritsa, Catherine, began to treat her badly since she had borne a son. The Tsaritsa and Menshikov systematically set my father against me— If left to himself, my father is kind and just, but he is extremely passionate—he believes that he, like God, has the right of life and death. He has shed much innocent blood—sometimes with his own hands. (pause) If the Emperor were to deliver me to my father, it would be certain death. Even if my father were to spare me, the Tsaritsa and Menshikov would not rest until they succeeded in killing me. The abdication of the throne has been extorted from me. I have no desire to become a monk. I have sufficient brains to govern. God is my witness, I never so much as contemplated rousing the people to revolt, though I could easily have done so, because the people are affectionate towards me, and dislike my father because of his unworthy wife, his debauched favorites, the desecration of the Churches, the abolition of old customs and because he is a BLOODY TYRANT!

Foreign Minister

Fear not, Your Highness; the Emperor will not forsake you. Should there be need of it after your father's death, he is prepared to help you to the throne with armed force.

Alexis

No! No! What are you talking about? I hope, for God's sake, it will never come to that. War will never be caused by me. It is not this I asked you for, only your protection. I am much obliged to you. May God reward the Emperor for the kindness he has shown me.

Foreign Minister

Our pilgrims have safely arrived in Naples. I will send my secretary at the very first opportunity with a very detailed description of the journey. Very entertaining. Our little page among other things, was discovered to be a woman, neither married and still less a maid. She is declared to be a mistress and indispensably necessary. Schonbrun reports that it is impossible to keep the young gentleman sober. Barbarians.

ACT III
SCENE 13

Alexis' quarters in Naples.

Alexis is writing. Afrossinia, fashionably dressed, is primping at a mirror.

Afrossinia

What are you at, Alexis?

Alexis

I am writing to my friends in Russia. "Honored gentlemen of the Senate, Your lordships are, no doubt, surprised at my unexplained absence. My flight was prompted by the way I have been persecuted and threatened with confinement to a monastery, without any misdeed on my part. At present, I am in good health, under the protection of an Emperor who is as just as he is powerful, until the time comes when the Lord who saved me commands me to return to Russia. I ask you to stand by me. Do not believe any report that I am not among the living. Alive by God's grace,

I remain, wishing you and the whole nation well.—" How do you like it?

Afrossinia (still regarding herself with evident satisfaction in a mirror)

Is it wise?

Alexis

There are some who are my friends. Look! (waving some papers) Here is a report from Pleyer. The regiments of the Guard have organized a plot in Mecklenburg. They propose killing the Tsar and shutting up Catherine with her three children in the same convent where my mother has been forced to stay for so many years.— Soon, dearest, all that you desire shall be at your disposal. This is good news! God will soon grant us a safe return.

Afrossinia (adjusting a beauty patch)

Alexis, suppose the Tsar is killed and you are sent for—will you side with the rebels?

Alexis

I don't know yet. Why build on probabilities? God's will be done. I only tell you this, Afrossinia, to show you how God works. My father plans one course, God follows his own!

Afrossinia

Which Senators will help you?

Alexis

And why should you trouble your head about it? Some pretend to be my enemy openly, the better to espouse my cause. Others are cowards hankering after my father's good will. I spit upon them all, if only the people are with me. When Tsar, I will turn all the old Senators out, and replace them with new ones—men of my own choice. My uncle, Abraham Lopoukhin writes that people of all ranks inquire after me, and sympathize with me. Everything is coming apart. No father, you won't have the best of it! The Swedes have landed troops in Lithuania and our main forces are far away. Petersburg lies within their reach. Petersburg will be destroyed! Destroyed!

(Afrossinia regards him calmly, indifferently.)

Alexis (disgusted, throwing down the papers he has been waving)

All this is idle talk. Nothing will ever come of it. The blue-jay spread his fame far and wide, yet when it came to action, he failed to set the world on fire.

Afrossinia

Hadn't I better go to bed, Alexis? I feel tired.

Alexis

Yes, my dear one—God protect you. I, too, may come after a while— Afrossinia dearest, aren't you glad? You will be queen and our child—he will be Tsar. We will call him Ivan.

Afrossinia

Nonsense. How can a serf girl become a Tsaritsa?

Alexis

Didn't father do the same? The woman who is now my father's wife used to wash linen.

Afrossinia

Nonsense.

Alexis (pulling her gown off, leaving her naked)

Come here.

Afrossinia

Let me go, Alexis. I am ashamed. Let me go.

Alexis

Afrossinia!

Afrossinia

Shame. On the eve of a Holy Day. Sin. Sin.

Alexis (pulling her to him)

My Tsaritsa! My Tsaritsa!

ACT III
SCENE 14

An audience hall in Naples.

Alexis is waiting, when Peter Tolstoi enters at a distance.

Alexis (jumping up)

It is he! He! He!

Foreign Minister (who has come in with Tolstoi)

Water! Water! The Tsarevitch is ill. Calm yourself, for God's sake. We bring the best of news.

Alexis (recovering himself)

How many came in?

Foreign Minister

Two, Your Highness—only two.

Alexis

I saw a third. I saw him. Where is he?

Foreign Minister

Who?

Alexis

My father! I saw him. I saw him as plainly as I see you now.

Tolstoi (stepping forward)

Dear me, had I but known that Your Highness was ill, I should not have requested the interview.

Alexis

You, Peter Tolstoi! I thought you were my father.

(Tolstoi is an aged, but well preserved fop. He is dressed in an elegant wig and fashionable waistcoat. Invariably, he takes snuff from an inlaid box.)

Alexis

Are you here to kill me?

Foreign Minister

Special precautions have been taken to frustrate any assault. I pledge my life and honor that no harm will come to you.

Tolstoi (bowing low)

Gracious Lord Tsarevitch, a letter from your father.

Alexis (cautiously taking the letter from Tolstoi and opening it)

I will listen.

Peter (appearing on the dais)

My son. It is generally known the disobedience and contempt of my will that you have shown me. Neither words nor fear of punishment can prevent you from pursuing your willfulness. You deceived me, and like a traitor, placed yourself under a stranger's protection. Having shamed your father and your country, I give you now one last chance to redeem yourself. Do as Count Tolstoi will tell you. (solemnly) If you do as I wish, I promise you, in the sight of God, that no punishment will be inflicted on you. I will show you even greater love if you obey and return to me. If you prefer to remain obstinate, then I, your father, will curse you and declare you a traitor. Remember, I have not used violence with you thus far. Had it been my intention to do so, I easily could bring you down. You know my power.

(Peter leaves the dais. Tolstoi approaches Alexis.)

Alexis (retreating)

Don't let him come any closer. (to Tolstoi) My father used to say of you that you were a clever man, but that in dealing with you it is wise to keep a club ready.

Tolstoi

Your father always has his little jokes. My Lord Tsarevitch, listen to your father's entreaties. He says: "If you do as I wish, I promise you, in the sight of God, that no punishment will be inflicted on you." He swore it on the relics. I have never known him to break his oath.

(Alexis remains silent. He knows his father is honorable.)

Tolstoi

He instructed me to tell you, (sighing) that should you refuse, he will pursue you with all the ample means in his power. If it must be, we will constrain the Emperor with armed force to give you up.

Alexis (scoffing)

Bah! My father will never wage war with the Emperor over me.

Tolstoi

I don't think it will be necessary. The Emperor will eventually give you up. He does not benefit from your stay here. He has fulfilled his promise towards you. He has protected you until you were pardoned and can freely return to Russia. His obligations are discharged. He will no longer shield you.

Alexis (to the Foreign Minister)

Is this true?

Foreign Minister

The Emperor has lately begun a war against the Turks and the Spaniards. Russia's neutrality is important. If this matter can be peaceably settled between you and your father, it will be to His Majesty's advantage. Should you find your father's propositions reasonable and his guarantees satisfactory, the Emperor would be pleased. Should you not, you may continue to enjoy his protection.

Alexis

How old are you, Peter Tolstoi?

Tolstoi (amiably)

Since there are no ladies present, I may confess that I am past seventy.

Alexis

According to the Scriptures, seventy is the limit of a man's life. How could you, Peter Tolstoi, with one foot in the grave, undertake such a mission as this? I always thought you had an affection for me.

Tolstoi

And so I do. Reconciling you to your father is my dearest wish.

Alexis

Don't tell lies, old man. Do you really think I don't know why you have been sent here? My father dispatched you to kill me.

Tolstoi

As God is my witness, Tsarevitch, it is not so. I would never undertake such a mission. Had your father wanted to kill you, he would have sent Menshikov. I am here as a peacemaker.

Alexis

You're a sly old fox, Peter Tolstoi, but no amount of honeyed words will lead this sheep into the wolf's jaws.

Tolstoi

You regard your father as a wolf?

Alexis

He's been one to me. And wolf or no, should I fall into his hands, not one of my bones will remain unbroken. You know the truth as well as I do.

Tolstoi

It is all very well to doubt me. But, see here!—in his own hand, he swears to God. Is it possible for him to break his oath in the sight of Europe.

Alexis (sneering)

What does he care for an oath? If it troubles his conscience, Theodosius will absolve him. He can do exactly what he pleases. He is God. No, Tolstoi, don't waste words. You won't get me alive.

Tolstoi (takes out a snuff box and unhurriedly takes a pinch, which he expertly "snuffs" first into one nostril, then the other)

There is nothing to be said then. Do as suits you best. You will not listen to me, maybe you will listen to your father. He will come as soon as he learns I have failed.

Alexis (astounded)

Here! It can't be! Are you lying again?

Tolstoi

I had no orders to inform you of it, or to conceal it. He wrote some time ago, informing me of his intentions. Who can prohibit a father from talking to his son?

Alexis

This is incredible. It's a nightmare. Why won't he leave me in peace?

Tolstoi

You know he's inexorable. Where can you hide yourself from your father? Only in the grave—he will find you everywhere else. I am sorry for you, my dear Alexis Petrovitch. Heartily sorry for you.

(Tolstoi turns to leave.)

Alexis

Wait, I want a word with the Foreign Minister before you go. (to the Minister) Suppose my father were to demand me with arms? Can I still depend on the Emperor's protection?

Foreign Minister

Don't be troubled, Your Highness; the Emperor is strong enough to defend those under his protection. It would be an inexcusable shame to him if he were forced to surrender a suppliant he had undertaken to protect.

Alexis

I know that, but will he do so? Leave politics alone. You see how I suffer.

Foreign Minister (hesitating)

I, I assure—

Alexis (falling on his knees)

I implore the Emperor, in the name of God and all the Saints, not to forsake me! It is awful even to think of what will happen if my father ever gets his powerful hands on me. No one else knows what manner of man he is. I know.

Foreign Minister (embarrassed)

Get up, Your Highness. I will tell you the plain truth. Nothing will induce the Emperor to return you to your father against your will. Such an act would be degrading to the honor of His Majesty.

Alexis (rising)

Thank you. Thank you. And if my father should come himself?

Foreign Minister

We could hardly deny him an audience, but that is all.

Alexis

My God! Don't you know how terrified I am, even to be in the same room with him? He can be like a wild beast. He executed the Strelsi with his own hands.

Foreign Minister

Calm yourself. The Emperor will protect you.

Alexis (pacing a bit)

Peter Tolstoi. I have decided to reply in writing to my father. At present, I can say nothing. I have to think.

Tolstoi

If Your Highness has any conditions, let me know them. I believe your father will consent to everything. Now is a good time to ask. He will even permit you to marry Afrossinia. We shall have time enough to talk. We have not met for the last time.

Alexis

There is nothing more to discuss. I will answer my father directly. There is no reason for you to stay. You can return to Russia.

Tolstoi

I am ordered not to leave this place without you. Should you leave this place, I must follow. (pause) Your father will not rest till he has got you, either dead or alive. This is your last hope for a reconciliation. (bowing) Your Lordship's most devoted servant.

(Tolstoi bows himself out.)

Alexis

Judas.

Foreign Minister

I regret to inform you that the Emperor insists you rid yourself of that woman you have with you. She must be sent away without further delay if you expect continued protection. I did not wish to tell you this in front of Count Tolstoi.

Alexis (stunned)

You know I can't give her up.

Foreign Minister

You must. She is causing a great scandal. Your father demands that she be given up as an evil influence on you.

Alexis

Why can't he leave me in peace? Why?

(Alexis throws himself on a couch in despair.)

ACT III
SCENE 15

Alexis' Apartment in Naples.

Afrossinia is alone, primping. She is very pregnant. Alexis bursts in.

Alexis

Get your things together. We go to the Pope tomorrow. He will receive us.

Afrossinia

Idle talk! If the Emperor refuses to lend his protection to a poor girl like me, how can the Pope do so? He has no army to protect me.

Alexis

Then, what can be done? The Emperor insists that I send you away. We must escape—escape at once.

Afrossinia

Escape, where? They'll catch us anywhere. Better return to your father.

Alexis

You, too, Afrossinia! Don't be misled with fairy tales.

Afrossinia

Count Tolstoi only wishes you good.

Alexis

Good? What do you know? Better hold your tongue. Women have long hair, but short wits. Do you hope to escape torture? Don't imagine it. Even your pregnancy will not protect you.

Afrossinia

But your father promised forgiveness—

Alexis (making a gesture of cutting his throat)

I know what that means. Should the Pope refuse, we go to France. Never mention it to me again, Afrossinia. Do you hear! Never!

Afrossinia (indifferently)

Well, the decision rests with you, Tsarevitch, only I won't go with you.

Alexis (stunned)

What is this?

Afrossinia (coolly)

I won't. I have already promised Count Tolstoi that I won't go anywhere with you—except to your father. You can go where you please, but not with me.

Alexis

Have you lost your mind? How could I live without you?

Afrossinia

Please yourself, Alexis, but I won't go. (obstinately) So don't bother to ask me.

Alexis

If I say you have to go, you have to go. Have you forgotten who you are?

Afrossinia (tartly)

I am a faithful servant of His Majesty, Tsar Peter. I will do as he commands. I will not go with you against your father's will.

Alexis (menacingly)

How much did he pay you? How much? Is this your gratitude to me? Viper, harlot!

Afrossinia

What is the good of reviling me, Tsarevitch? I will do as I say. If they ask me to, I shall leave you.

Alexis

You won't do it. You can't do this to me, and to our child!

Afrossinia

You think, perhaps, I love you? You took me by force, by a master's right. You threatened me with a knife.

Alexis

Only to ease your conscience. Besides, haven't I made it up to you? I promise you, I'll marry you. You know I already treat you as my wife. And far better than I did my lawful one.

Afrossinia (mockingly)

Thank your lordship for his gracious favor. (curtsies) Marry you! I'd as soon be hanged. I wish you'd killed me that time. You raped me! You think I forget. You killed your wife, neglected your children and fell at the feet of a woman you have made into a whore. Look at yourself. A woman insults you, and you remain silent. I treat you like a dog, yet I need only whistle and you'll be panting after me like a dog after a bitch. With your tongue hanging out. Is it possible to love a thing like you? As for your brat, the moment it is born, I will strangle it with my own hands.

(Alexis puts his hands over his ears. Afrossinia walks to an escritoire and begins to write.)

Afrossinia

"Count Tolstoi, please come for me, immediately, or else he will carry me away by force."

Alexis (snatching the letter)

So it IS to HIM!

Afrossinia

I will do just as I like. I am not required to consult you about where I am to go.

Alexis (grabbing her hair and throwing her down)

You BITCH!

(Alexis begins to strangle her and she faints. Horrified, he slowly comes to himself.)

Alexis (sobbing)

I have killed her—killed her— Lord Jesus, take my life for her life.

(Alexis tries desperately and succeeds in reviving her.)

Alexis

Afrossinia! Afrossinia, are you all right?

Afrossinia (tenderly)

You thought you'd finished me, eh? It's not quite so easy to kill a woman. We have nine lives, like a cat.

Alexis (contritely)

Forgive me, forgive me, Afrossinia.

Afrossinia

A lover's blow does no harm. Foolish boy, you believed I don't love you. (low) I love you as my own soul. Do you believe me now?

Alexis

I believe you, I believe you.

Afrossinia

God gave me a grasping heart. I see you love me, but that's not enough. I want more. I wanted to see if you loved me. Really loved me. You nearly killed me—So now I know you do—. You think I cannot caress. You'll see how I can love. (she utters a throaty laugh) Only do what I ask. Then I shall know you love me as I love you—UNTO DEATH.

Alexis (spellbound)

I will do anything you ask.

Afrossinia (caressing him passionately)

Return to your father. I am sick unto death of being a fugitive. I want to be your wife. You say I am your wife now. What sort of wife? Our son will be born a bastard. Go to your father—go to your father, but, on the condition you are allowed to marry. This is all I want, .Alexis.

Alexis (ready to go to his doom for her)

I'll do it.

Afrossinia

Even if it means your death!

Alexis (resolutely)

I will!

Afrossinia

Swear it!

Alexis

I swear before God!

(Afrossinia blows out the candles and hurls herself on him in a kind of erotic fury.)

Alexis (passionately)

Sorceress! Witch! What have you done?

(They lock in an embrace as the scene ends. They hold their pose as Tolstoi enters addressing Peter who appears on the dais.)

Tolstoi

It is truly amazing, Your Highness. All his former stubbornness is gone. He asks only that he be allowed to wed Afrossinia before reaching Petersburg. And though his condition is rather tiresome, I have taken the liberty of granting it on my own accord without awaiting your order. If there is no special reason against it, let him have his way. In that way, he will show the world what kind of man he is. Secondly, it will annoy the Emperor to the degree that we may never need worry of his intervening on your son's behalf again. It will be a long journey because the wench is pregnant and he will not travel fast out of consideration for her. It is impossible to describe how he loves her, and with what solicitude he watches over her. Incidentally, she deserves some consideration, as she has cooperated with us in persuading him to return—although I am not sure what her motivations were in doing so. God alone knows the difficulties that have arisen over this affair. I cannot tell you the miracles we have accomplished.

(Peter signifies satisfaction and assent to all Tolstoi's report and actions and descends from the dais. Tolstoi takes snuff with great satisfaction from his beautiful snuff box.)

Tolstoi

Not bad work for an old man.

CURTAIN

ACT IV
SCENE 16

Peter before an altar, praying.

Peter

If a son so braves his father in his father's lifetime, what will he not do after his death? Will he not destroy and scatter everything? Will there be one stone left in the house I have built? He will ruin Russia. No—better break the oath than pardon! (pause) If I forgive him, must I not forgive all other traitors to Tsar and country? Yet, if I kill him—in one scale will be placed whatever good I have done; in the other, the death of my son. Will all my glory be tarnished by this stain of blood? Who—who does not know the provocation I have suffered and will discern my innocence? I am alone before God. Lord deliver me from blood guilt— (he kneels and bows in prayer) When I was executing the Strelsi rebels, the Patriarch met me, icon in hand, imploring me to pardon them. I bowed before the icon but pushed the old man aside. I said, "I revere the Virgin as much as you. But duty bids me pardon the just and punish the guilty. Go, old man!" I answered the Patriarch, but what answer shall I make to you, O God? Dear God, what is your will?

(Peter remains before the altar praying, perplexed, and deeply troubled.)

ACT IV
SCENE 17

Peter's apartment in Peterhof.

Tolstoi and Alexis are awaiting the Tsar. Alexis grips Tolstoi's hand.

Alexis

Peter Andreitch! Peter Andreitch! What will happen? I confess I am afraid.

Tolstoi

Courage, Your Highness. A sin confessed is half forgiven. Everything will arrange itself.

Alexis (mumbling)

Father, I can justify nothing. I only pray for your forgiveness. I give myself up to your hands.

Tolstoi

Never forget he loves you.

Alexis (listening)

I hear his step.

Tolstoi

Never forget, mind.

Peter (enters)

Welcome, Aliosha, thank the Lord! Thank the Lord, we have met at last— (he stretches his arm to meet him)

Alexis (embracing his father)

Forgive me, father. Forgive. Forgive.

Peter

Aliosha, my boy, quiet, quiet.

(Peter, with a gesture, bids Tolstoi begone. Peter is genuinely glad to see his son again. There should be no question of hypocrisy, notwithstanding Tolstoi's exiting remark.)

Tolstoi (exiting)

Thus the hawk will kiss the chicken till the last feather is gone.

Peter (goes to a table and pours liquor into two glasses)

Your health, Aliosha. (they clink glasses and drink)

Alexis

I've stopped drinking, you know.

Peter

That's wonderful. Even a dark cloud has a silver lining. (pause) You've grown thin abroad. Wait a bit, we'll soon fill you out. Russian bread is better feeding than German, you know. (pouring) Have another. (they drink again)

Alexis

You know about Afrossinia...?

Peter

Your taste isn't bad. Afrossinia is a strapping—a superb wench; were I ten years younger, you might have cause to be jealous. Apples don't fall far from the tree. Father with a washerwoman, son with a charwoman. But, what of it, eh? Katrinka washed clothes. Do you want to get married, still?

Alexis

Very much, if you permit it, father.

Peter

What else can I do? I promised you, I can't help myself now. (pours again) To peace and eternal friendship. (they clink and drink) (touching Aliosha's hand) Tell me, Aliosha, tell me—all about your flight.

Alexis

I will tell you everything, only forgive them all as you have forgiven me.

Peter (laying his hands on his son's shoulders)

How can I forgive if I don't know what has been done. I can forgive so far as I myself am concerned, but not a crime against Russia. I will pardon all those you name, but terrible penalties will fall on all those you conceal. Don't be afraid, I will hurt no one. We will talk it over between us.

(Alexis remains silent, troubled. Peter presses his son's hand against his breast.)

Peter

Aliosha, Aliosha, if only you knew my heart. I have no one to help me. I am always alone. Be my friend. Or don't you love me?

Alexis (with great feeling)

I love you, dearest father. Only I am afraid.

Peter

Speak, it will ease you. Speak out as in confession.

Alexis

When you were ill, I thought you would not live. I wished you dead.

Peter (pushing him back and looking directly in his eyes)

Did you plot my death with anyone?

Alexis

No, no, no!

Peter (after studying Alexis)

Well—it is so. I believe you. All will be well—

Alexis

I know, father, it may be impossible for you to forgive me. So be it. Have me killed. I will die for you. Only love me. Love me always. Let no one know about all this. You and I alone will know, you and I—

(Peter takes Alexis' head between his hands and kisses him.)

Alexis

Father, you're weeping.

Peter

It will be all right. So, I have a son. Now, you must tell me everything—all the names.

Alexis

Ask me—but do not hurt them.

Peter

It will be as I said. We will talk it all over between us.

(Peter embraces his son and leads him from the room.)

ACT IV
SCENE 18

An audience hall in the Peterhof Palace.

Peter is seated on a throne. Alexis, accompanied by Tolstoi and two guards enter.

Tolstoi

Kneel! Kneel! Speak, as you have prepared.

Alexis

Most gracious sovereign and father! On recognizing my sin towards you as parent and sovereign, I wrote a letter to you, begging your forgiveness. Today, I repeat and declare that, forgetful of my duties as a son and subject, I deserted Russia. For which transgression I beg your gracious pardon and forgiveness.

Tolstoi (reading a decree)

"We trust that it is known to all our faithful subjects how carefully we have striven to bring up our first-born son, Alexis. But all our efforts were in vain—our son hated study and has shown no interest for civil or military affairs, preferring intercourse with worthless reactionaries."

Alexis (to himself)

I still know you love me.

Tolstoi (reading)

"Seeing his obstinacy, we declared that, should he not mend his ways, we would disinherit him. But he, forgetful of all responsibility and God's law which commands obedience to parents, was ungrateful and fled—deserted to the Emperor in Vienna. There he spread many untrue calumnies against us and brought dishonor to us and great shame— before all the world. It is difficult to find a precedent for it in history. Yet, though he has, by these deeds, earned death—we pity him with our fatherly heart, forgive, and free him of all punishment. But—"

Peter (angrily breaking in)

I cannot have an heir who would waste all that his father, with God's help, has gained. I should fear to meet my God if I entrusted the government to one I knew to be unfit for it. And you— (to Alexis) And you remember this: though I have pardoned you, yet, if you have made a single omission or reservation which comes out later, do not reproach me,—it will cost you your pardon. You shall suffer death— (Peter subsides, and after a look at Peter, Tolstoi resumes reading the decree)

Tolstoi

"Thus, in our anxiety for our subjects, we herewith, by reason of our power as father and absolute sovereign, take from our son Alexis the right to succeed to the Russian throne even if no other member of our family should survive us. And we herewith appoint and declare our son Peter, though yet a child, heir to the throne."

Peter

Bring the cross.

(The Archbishop Theodosius and several other prelates bring a cross forward and a document.)

Peter

Read, then sign the abdication.

Alexis (reading)

"I, Alexis Petrovitch Romanoff, promise on the Holy Gospels that I, having forfeited my inheritance of the Russian throne, acknowledge the forfeiture to be just, and swear, by the Almighty God, to submit to my father's will without fail and never seek the succession, nor to accept it under any pretext whatever. I acknowledge my brother Peter to be the legitimate heir. Upon which I kiss the cross and sign with my own hand." (he kisses the cross and signs, the prelates step back)

Tolstoi (reading)

"All those who from this day forth, contrary to our desire, persist in regarding Alexis heir to the throne, we herewith declare traitors to us and Russia."

(There is a roll of drums. The spectators withdraw.)

Peter

Did you hear what has just been said before the people? One concealment will cost you your life.

Alexis

I have heard it, father.

Peter

And have you nothing to add to what you have declared yesterday?

Alexis

Nothing.

Peter

Are you sure there is nothing? If you tell me now, I will forgive you still.

Alexis

Nothing.

Peter

You lie. You have concealed all about your mother, your aunt, your uncle and their whole cursed brood. The root of all this wicked rebellion.

Alexis (dryly)

Who told you, father?

Peter

Is it not true?

Alexis

Forgive, forgive! She is my mother. She bore me. I could not more betray her than I could betray you.

(Peter raises his fist, but Alexis falls to his knees and clings to his father's legs.)

Alexis

Don't go away. Don't. Rather, kill me.

Peter

Release me, or I'll kill you.

(Alexis does not release Peter, but Peter shakes him off and leaves Alexis sprawled on the floor.)

Tolstoi

Are you all right, Alexis Petrovitch? Perhaps, some water?

Alexis

Who told my father?

Tolstoi (evasively)

I cannot say.

Alexis

Tell me.

Tolstoi

There is an unpublished decree that requires any priest who receives knowledge of a plot against the Tsar to report it at once to the secret police. Even if he learned of it in confession.

Alexis

I confessed last night. God—he has brought the Church to this. To the role of informers. He is not Tsar, but a werewolf.

ACT IV
SCENE 19

A Cathedral.

Archbishop Theodosius is concluding a sermon invoking a blessing on the new heir. Peter and Alexis and several others look on.

Theodosius

Rejoice, O Russia, be proud and thankful. Let all thy cities be glad, for like a sun, the true heir, Peter Petrovitch, shines on you. May he live happily, may he reign prosperously, Peter the Second, Peter the blessed! Amen.

Voice: Lord save, keep and bestow thy grace upon the only true heir to the Russian throne, the most pious Tsarevitch, Alexis Petrovitch.

Peter (menacingly)

Who said that? Who dared?

Dokoukin (stepping forward)

I did, Your Highness.

(Peter is interested, he admires courage)

Dokoukin

Larion Dokoukin, formerly a clerk in the arsenal.

Peter (calmly)

Do you refuse to swear allegiance?

Dokoukin

I will swear allegiance to you, but not to Tsarevitch Peter because of the unmerited expulsion of the only legitimate heir, Lord Alexis Petrovitch! May God keep him. Amen! Amen! Amen!

Peter

Old man, do you know that such disobedience to our will means death?

Dokoukin

I know it, Lord. I came with the view of suffering for Christ's sake.

Peter

You are a brave old man. But will you be so brave on the gallows? Do you believe me to be Tsar?

Dokoukin

I do.

Peter

Then you should do as we wish and hold your tongue.

Dokoukin (falling at Peter's feet)

Lord Tsar, Your Majesty, hold my tongue, even if I would, I cannot. I burn inwardly like a flame. Listen to us miserable people. We, too, want to be saved and reach the heavenly city. We dare not change and alter everything but must seek God in the same way as our fathers and their fathers before them. The way the Holy Patriarchs set out is the only sure way. Do not set everything at naught. In the name of God and Jesus, leave us as we are. Show mercy unto thy people.

Peter

Enough! Enough. Do you imagine that I revere God less than you? Who set you slaves to judge between God and Tsar?

Dokoukin

It is said in the Holy Scriptures "What is man, that Thou art mindful of him?" Thus it is that God has ordained man to be lord of himself. What have you made of him?

Peter

Take him to prison.

Dokoukin

The powers that be are ordained by God and what is not of God is no power. It is not fitting to call impious Tsars and Antichrists the anointed of God.

Peter (interested)

Do you consider me Antichrist? Speak the truth.

Dokoukin (fearlessly)

None other. O secret martyrs, fear not, neither despair! Bear patiently yet a while for the Lord's sake. Antichrist's power is waning. His rule will be short. Jesus is coming. He will not be slow. Even so! Come Lord Jesus. Amen.

Peter

Take him away. No doubt I have hanged too few such

fools.

(Dokoukin is led out by guards. Peter exits with his entourage.)

Alexis (lagging behind)

That man is as I should be.

ACT IV
SCENE 20

A small room in the Peterhof.

It is furnished in a Dutch style. Peter is seated at a table writing. Alexis either stands or sits before him.

Peter

Who among the clergy or laity knew anything of your revolutionary designs and what words passed between you on the subject?

Alexis

I know nothing beyond what I have already admitted.

Peter

Have you ever said, "I spit upon them all, provided the mob is with me?"

Alexis

Possibly. I was drunk most of the time, and I can't

remember everything— But what does it matter? (smiling)

Peter (regarding his son with horror)

Is this your handwriting?

Alexis (examining a document Peter has handed him)

It is.

Peter (quietly)

You beseech the Prelates and Senators not to abandon you?

Alexis

Yes.

Peter (horrified)

Did you write this of your own free will?

Alexis

No. They told me that it was rumored that I was dead. If I refused to write along these lines, the Emperor would no longer protect me.

Peter

It reads, "I beseech you NOW, not to abandon me NOW." The word now is twice repeated and then scratched out. Why had you written the word "now?"

Alexis (hesitant)

I can no longer remember. Perhaps it was an error.

Peter

Has this been written under pressure?

Alexis

Yes, certainly.

Peter

You swear it?

Alexis

Before God.

(Peter rings a bell and Afrossinia enters. Alexis moves to embrace Afrossinia but is checked by his father's gaze.)

Peter

Is it true, Afrossinia, that the Tsarevitch was compelled to write this letter to the Bishops and the Senators?

Afrossinia

It is false. He was alone with me when he wrote it.

Alexis

Afrossinia! Afrossinia! What are you saying? (to Peter) She knows nothing. It was another letter she remembers—she's mixed up.

Afrossinia (defiantly)

The very same, Tsarevitch. You wrote and sealed it in my presence.

Peter

This is a matter of grave importance. If this letter was voluntarily written, it is clear that your projects for rebellion were not vague. You counted on being able to put them into execution. You passed over this, not through forgetfulness, but of a set purpose that you might be forgiven and continue your schemes. However, I do not wish to bear an uneasy conscience and accept an accusation without full enquiry. It is evident Afrossinia bears you a grudge of some kind— For the last time, I ask you, did you write it of your own free will?

(Alexis is silent.)

Peter

Very well. I regret the necessity, Afrossinia, but you must be handed over to official interrogation.

Alexis

Torture?

Peter

You know the procedures.

Alexis (low)

I confess it.

Peter (joyfully)

So! (pause) For what purpose did you write the word "now?"

Alexis

So as to signal the people to rise.

Peter

And had they been so misguided as to rise, you would

have joined them?

Alexis

If they sent for me. I expected a summons after your death.

Peter

And if I did not die?

Alexis (savagely)

If I had had the people with me in sufficient force, even during your lifetime, I should have laid claim to the empire!

Peter (stunned at first by his son's outburst, he pauses, then turns to Afrossinia, speaking in a shaky voice for the first and only time in the play)

Declare all you know.

Afrossinia (repeating as if from a memorized speech)

The Tsarevitch has always ardently desired to rule. He ran away because he pretended to fear Your Majesty was plotting to kill him. When he heard your youngest son was ill, he said to me, "You see my father takes his own course, while God wills another." He used to read prophecies and say, "Either my father will die, or a rebellion will break out." When Tolstoi arrived in

Naples, the Tsarevitch wanted to flee to the Pope.

Peter (with recovered composure)

Is all this true?

Alexis

It is.

Peter

You may go now, Afrossinia. Thank you!

(Afrossinia kisses the Tsar's hand, curtsies, and abruptly turns her back on Alexis who stretches his hand towards her. She leaves the room with a firm, decisive step.)

Alexis

Afrossinia! Afrossinia. (she does not turn) Farewell then, love of my life. We shall not meet again. The Lord be with you. (to Peter) Why do you treat me like this? (Peter does not respond and shuffles some papers with affected indifference. Suddenly, Alexis hides his head in his hands.) What have you done with the child? Where is it? What has happened to it?

Peter (not understanding)

What child?

Alexis (pointing to the door)

Our child!

Peter

It is dead. It never lived.

Alexis (rising up with clenched fists)

That is a lie! You have killed it.

(Peter avoids his son's eyes and remains silent.)

Alexis

Was it a boy?

Peter

Yes.

Alexis

Did you have it strangled or did you drown it?

Peter

The child was stillborn.

Alexis

If God had granted me to rule, I would have made him

my heir. I meant to call him Ivan. The body, where is it? What have you done with it? Speak!

(Peter remains silent.)

Alexis (cunningly, with a slightly insane intonation)

I know, I know. You've sealed him in a glass jar with spirits of wine—like a frog. The heir of the Tsars of Russia, swimming like a preserved frog.

Peter

Are you mad, or simply playing the fool? What else have you got to confess? If you reckoned on support of the people, did you not send envoys to prepare them for the rising—?

(Alexis remains silent, lost in his own thoughts.)

Peter (convulsed with rage)

Speak!

Alexis (decisively)

I have told you everything I shall ever tell you. I shall say no more.

Peter (striking the table with his fist)

How dare you?

Alexis (rising, looking steadily at his father)

Why use threats, father? I am not afraid of you. I fear nothing. You have taken everything from me. You have destroyed everything in me. It only remains for you to kill me. Do so. I am quite indifferent.

(Peter rises in a fury and hurls himself on Alexis, striking him with his cane. Alexis offers no resistance. Catherine enters hurriedly and restrains Peter.)

Peter

Have I killed him?

(The lights dim, with Peter standing over the prostrate body of his son. Then, Tolstoi comes forward.)

Tolstoi

It has been decided that the Tsarevitch shall be tried in the High Court as a traitor. It is true the Tsar had promised to grant his son a pardon, on the understanding that he sincerely repented of his misdeeds; but, since Alexis, in contempt of this proffered favor, has concealed a plot to make himself Tsar and to usurp the throne, the pardon is hereby annulled and cancelled.

ACT IV
SCENE 21

Peter's apartments.

Several Priests appear on the dais, headed by Theodosius. Peter turns to them.

Peter

Most Reverend Metropolitans, Archbishops, Bishops and other members of the clergy.

You are acquainted with the unprecedented transgressions of my son against me, his father and sovereign. I, as autocrat, possess full power, moral and judicial, to deal with him according to my own will, without consulting others. Yet, I fear to sin before God. I do not wish to act from passion or anger. A doctor does not prescribe for his own ailment. In like manner do I now confide to your care this malady of mine.

I swore before God to my son, both by letter and word of mouth, to pardon him if he made a full confession of his guilt. And, though he broke the agreement by concealing his projected rebellion against me, his father and Tsar, yet, it is our will, that you, the Clergy, search the Scriptures for some indication of the punishment befitting our son.

(The Clergy pivot to and fro, stand on one leg, now another, nod and bow to each other, and gyrate in argument. Then Theodosius speaks.)

Theodosius

Most gracious sovereign and Tsar. After deep consultation in the scripture and with doctors of canon law, it is our conclusion that this is a case for the civil, not the spiritual tribunal. He, in whom the sovereign power resides, cannot be judged by his subjects. This matter is not within our province. We propose that the sovereign act in this matter as he may think best. Should he desire to chastise the guilty, he has the example of the Old Testament. If he desires to show grace, he has the example of Christ himself who pardoned the prodigal son. In short, the monarch's heart is in the hand of God. Amen.

All the Clergy Amen. Amen.

(Alexis, listening to this response, doubles over with laughter.)

Alexis

Spiritual diplomats. Ha, ha, ha.

Peter (in consternation)

But, what of my oath?

(The Clergy make a profound obeisance and withdraw from the dais.)

Peter

I fear damnation.

Alexis

Ha, ha, ha. My father has the spiritual comfort he has earned. Ha, ha, ha.

ACT IV
SCENE 22

The Senate.

Several tiers of benches. A throne for the Tsar at the right. Peter does not sit in the throne, but in a chair beside it. The Tsarevitch is led in by two officers with drawn swords.

Tolstoi

The court is open.

Peter (addressing the Senate)

Gentlemen of the Senate, I pray you to judge this case in the fullest spirit of equity. It is too serious to consider favoritism or flattery. If you believe a light punishment will suffice, but hesitate through fear of my displeasure, I pledge that this will not be incurred. I pray you also to give no weight to the consideration that it is the son of the Tsar you are called upon to judge. Imperil in no wise your souls or mine. Let the rights of men and man prevail.

Tolstoi

You know the charges, Tsarevitch?

Alexis

I do.

Tolstoi

Do you plead guilty?

Alexis

Whether I be guilty or not is not for you, but for God alone to judge. How is it possible for you to pass righteous judgment, when you yourselves are slaves? Whatever he bids you say or do, you do or say. Your tribunal is a tribunal of wolves. Were I innocent a hundred times over, you would condemn me. If, instead of you, it was the Russian people proceeding against me, that would be an entirely different matter. I love the people. Peter is great—very great—but his rule is stern. What lives have been lost, how much blood has been shed to turn Russians into Frenchmen and Germans? Do you hear nothing? Do you see nothing? The earth groans beneath his feet.

(A murmur of disapproval.)

Voices Hush! Treason! Foolish boy. Stop his mouth.

Alexis

Why are you silent, father? Does it startle you to hear the truth? Had you merely ordered my head cut off I would not have said a word; but, since you have instituted this mock tribunal, whether you like it or not, you shall hear. When you lured me back to Petersberg with the aid of that Judas (pointing to Tolstoi) did you not swear to God to pardon me everything? What account do you give of that promise? You are dishonored before Russia and the world. The autocrat of Russia—a common perjurer and liar—

Voices

He has lost his mind. Away with him. He is condemning himself. Silence. Hush.

(Tolstoi goes to Peter and whispers in his ear, but Peter sits expressionless—as if dead. Tolstoi looks on with great perplexity.)

Alexis

You shall be the first to stain the block with the blood of a son. The blood of Russia's Tsars. This blood will descend for successive generations to the last Tsar—all shall perish in blood. God will visit your sin upon Russia.

Peter (rising)

Silence! Silence! I will curse you.

Alexis (with great indignation)

You will curse me? (rushing towards his father with clenched fists) You will curse me! I, myself, will curse you— Villain— Murderer! Beast, Antichrist. Be accursed, accursed, accursed!

(Peter starts up in a rage, then collapses in a faint.)

Tolstoi (frantically)

The session is closed. The session is closed.

ACT IV
SCENE 23

Peter's apartments.

Peter is pacing furiously, Tolstoi waits patiently.

Tolstoi (puzzled)

What is the use of putting him to further torture? He has disclosed everything.

Peter

There is more! Much more.

Tolstoi (shrugs)

Perhaps, if I were to talk to him.

Peter

Go today. After Mass. Question him on the following points. Ask him why he has refused to act according to the least of my wishes? Why he has felt neither shame nor remorse? Why he has sought to win his inheritance by disobeying me?

Tolstoi

Excuse me, Highness, but it seems to me that these are not questions worth pursuing at great length.

Peter

I must know. He must answer me. If I am not satisfied on these points, I will lose my mind— (Tolstoi shrugs in a way as to suggest that in his opinion Peter has already lost his mind) Go.

Tolstoi

I shall endeavor.

ACT IV
SCENE 24

Alexis' cell.

Alexis lies on a cot. Tolstoi enters.

Alexis (dreaming)

Send her away, for God's sake, send her away. Don't you see her there, mewing like a cat? The cursed thing that caresses! She will fly at my throat, and tear my heart out with her claws. (seeing Tolstoi) What do you what of me?

Tolstoi

Your father sent me.

Alexis

Again, to torture me. I know nothing more.

Tolstoi

Fear nothing.

Alexis

Leave me alone. Kill me, only don't torture me again! If you are afraid, give me a razor, I will do it myself. Only be quick. Be quick!

Tolstoi (gently)

Come, come, be calm. I am not a torturer. Torturing you was no idea of mine. If God be willing, all may come right. The world is full of strange events. You may yet win a reprieve. (pause) Do you think I do not pity you?

Alexis

Then, why did you lure me back?

Tolstoi

I am a diplomat, and a faithful servant of the state. In a word it was my job—

(Alexis spits at him.)

Tolstoi (not resenting this)

I pity you with all my heart. I have always wished you well, and today, still.

Alexis

Go away. (spits again) That for your good wishes.

Tolstoi

Your father demands answers to certain questions.

Alexis

I know nothing more.

Tolstoi

Excuse me, I know that's true, Tsarevitch, but obtaining answers to these questions has become a fixed idea with your father. If you fail to answer him, I can only predict the worst.

Alexis (wearily)

What are your questions?

Tolstoi

"Why do you disobey him?" "Why do you feel no remorse or fear?" "Why do you seek to win your inheritance by disobedience?"

Alexis (puzzled)

But, I hardly know myself. What difference does it

make?—

Tolstoi

Excuse me, Tsarevitch, it makes every difference. Your father is tormented by these questions. Personally, I think he has gone a little mad. It is certainly driving him crazy, if he is not so already.

Alexis (amused)

It bothers him, does it?

Tolstoi

He is inexorable.

Alexis

What further answer can I make? I am Alexis, he is Peter. Let him suffer in ignorance—or search his own heart.

Tolstoi

That will never do. If only you could satisfy him, all might be put right. I have thought much about it. If you will write, I will dictate.

Alexis

No. Not unless you obtain permission for me to see

Afrossinia.

Tolstoi

I will do that. You shall see Afrossinia. Perhaps you will be pardoned and even allowed to marry her. Only write. Write.

(Tolstoi places writing materials before Alexis. Tolstoi starts the first paragraph and Alexis completes it.)

Tolstoi

"One. My insubordination to my father comes from being brought up by ignorant women."

Alexis (writing)

"They made a fanatic of me. Study was hateful to me. I worked most lazily. Since my father was absent for prolonged periods, these women observed that I took pleasure in talking to priests and monks. They encouraged that inclination. They also knew I liked Vodka and they encouraged that vice as well. Little by little, they estranged me more and more from my father, and urged me in every way to resist him in all things, working on both my good instincts (my religion) and my bad (my drunkenness)."

Tolstoi

Very good. Very good. It may work. "Two. My lack of

remorse is explained by a naturally weak disposition."

Alexis

"It was also the result of constant encouragement that I was in the right in opposing my father's reforms at every step. I had become the pawn of a reactionary clique."

Tolstoi

"Three. As to why I thought to obtain power other than through obedience—"

Alexis

"It was because my father was beyond imitation; I knew myself incapable of following in his path, therefore, out of jealousy, I chose to usurp the throne." There. I am done.

Tolstoi

Very good. I think it may work. Let us hope it will appease him.

Alexis

It will not. It is my death warrant. But, take it. The truth is worse still.

(Tolstoi bows and leaves.)

ACT IV
SCENE 25

Alexis' cell.

Alexis is in his cot. Suddenly Alexis starts up screaming.

Alexis

There, see how she lies in wait for me! Her eyes are just like two blazing coals, her whiskers bristle just like my father's! Get away.

(Father Matthew enters hesitantly and stands by the cot.)

Alexis

Who are you?

Matthew

The priest of the garrison. I have been sent to receive your confession.

Alexis

To receive my confession? Why do you bear a calf's head on your shoulders and shaggy hair on your face—and horns? Why, eh?

Matthew

Do you desire to confess, my lord Tsarevitch?

Alexis

Are your acquainted, priest—if that is what you are—with my father's Ukase by and which all treason or seditious plots—even if revealed in confession, must be disclosed to the secret police?

Matthew

I know of it, Your Highness.

Alexis

And, should I reveal something of this kind, would you betray me?

Matthew

How could I help it? I have a wife and children.

Alexis

Away,—get away from me! Slave of the Tsar. You are sold down to the last man. You have delivered the Church to the Antichrist. I will receive no sacrament from your hands! Begone!

(Father Matthew leaves hurriedly.)

Alexis

Now, pretty kitty. Come back. I'm ready for you now.

ACT IV
SCENE 26

Outside Alexis' cell.

Peter, Doctor and the Executioner are conferring.

Peter

Weakling, shrimp. Why won't he tell the truth? Why does he still defy me?

Doctor

He must not be beaten any more, Your Majesty. He may die of it. Besides, it is quite useless, he is in a state of catalepsy and can feel nothing.

Peter

What?

Doctor

Catalepsy is a state—

Peter

You are in a catalepsy yourself, fool! (to the Executioner) And you. You dawdle. Strike as hard as you can. Or have you forgotten how flogging is done?

Executioner

I do my work in the Russian way. I have not learned from foreigners. It is so easy to kill. He scarcely breathes, poor fellow. He is not a beast, after all, but a Christian.

Peter (rushing at him)

You just wait, you devil's son. I will teach you how to strike.

Executioner

Do what pleases Your Majesty. I will not strike another blow.

(Peter snatches the knout which the executioner throws down and rushes into the cell.)

ACT IV
SCENE 27

The Emperor's Palace in Vienna.

The Foreign Minister is making his report to the Emperor.

Foreign Minister

All things will one day end in Russia in some fearful revolution. The autocracy will fall because the people cry out against the Tsar. The Crown Prince died, not of apoplexy, as is officially reported, but of a sword or axe. No one was admitted to the fortress on the day of his death. A Dutch Carpenter who remained in the fortress after completing some repairs, remained over night. He saw strange men enter the Prince's cell. The body of the Prince was laid in a coffin of inferior make; the head was partly covered, while a handkerchief was wound round the neck for shaving.

Peter (appearing on the dais)

After the pronouncement of the verdict on our son, we,

his father, assailed by pity on one side, and the desire to assure our country's peace on the other, could not come to a decision all at once on this highly difficult matter. Yet, it pleased God to deliver us from this difficulty and to preserve the empire from danger. Yesterday, on June 26, our son was taken from this life; when the verdict and the list of crimes was being read to him, the Tsarevitch was seized with a kind of apoplexy. He recovered consciousness and received the last rites of the Church. He also asked us to come to him, and we, disregarding all the trouble he had caused us, went to him. He confessed all his faults, and, shedding abundant tears of repentance, begged our forgiveness, which we readily granted him. Thus, he died as a Christian and as a repentant son. Our sorrow is inexpressible.

(Peter retires from the dais.)

Foreign Minister

Most people do not believe that pious fairy tale. Some asserted he had died under his father's blows. Others said he had not died. A few years later, there appeared among the Yemen Cossacks, a certain Timofee, the Worker. He claimed to be Alexis. He went through the steppes collecting an Army, promising to discover the city which held the insignia of the Virgin Mary, and the True Cross. He swore that he, Alexis Petrovitch, would reign and that, when Antichrist appeared, he would defeat him and all his evil spirits. The worker was arrested, tortured, and executed as a pretender. But the people go on believing in the Tsarevitch Alexis. Thus, even after his death, Alexis remained for the people, "Russia's hope."

Voice of Alexis

You are the first to stain the block with the blood of a son, the blood of Russia's Tsars; this blood shall descend for successive generations of thy lineage unto the last Tsar; all will perish in blood. God will visit your sin upon Russia.

Peter (appearing alone on the dais)

Not this, O Lord. Let it not be so. Let his blood come upon me, me alone! Punish me, O God! Spare Russia.

(Peter is alone as the curtain falls.)

CURTAIN

ABOUT THE AUTHOR

Frank J. Morlock has written and translated many plays since retiring from the legal profession in 1992. His translations have also appeared on Project Gutenberg, the Alexandre Dumas Père web page, Literature in the Age of Napoléon, Infinite Artistries.com, and Munsey's (formerly Blackmask). In 2006 he received an award from the North American Jules Verne Society for his translations of Verne's plays. He lives and works in México.

www.ingramcontent.com/pod-product-compliance
Lightning Source LLC
LaVergne TN
LVHW041623070426
835507LV00008B/410